MY VINYL COLLECTION

HOW TO BUILD, MAINTAIN, AND EXPERIENCE A MUSIC COLLECTION IN ANALOG

JENNA MILES

ADAMS MEDIA
New York London Toronto
Sydney New Delhi

Adams Media
An Imprint of Simon & Schuster, Inc.
100 Technology Center Drive
Stoughton, Massachusetts 02072

First Adams Media trade paperback edition November 2022

Interior design by
Colleen Cunningham
Interior images © 123RF/Ilya Bolotov
Interior illustrations by Eric Andrews

Manufactured in the United States of America

1 2022

Library of Congress Cataloging-in-Publication Data
Names: Miles, Jenna, author.
Title: My vinyl collection / Jenna Miles.
Description: First Adams Media trade paperback edition. | Stoughton, Massachusetts: Adams Media, 2022.
Identifiers: LCCN 2022027885 | ISBN 9781507219959 (pb)
Subjects: LCSH: Sound recordings--Collectors and collecting. | Phonograph. | Sound recordings--History.
Classification: LCC ML1055 .M46 2022 | DDC 780.26/6--dc23/eng/20220613
LC record available at https://lccn.loc.gov/2022027885

ISBN 978-1-5072-1995-9

Contains material adapted from the following title published by Adams Media, an Imprint of Simon & Schuster, Inc.: *The Beginner's Guide to Vinyl* by Jenna Miles, copyright © 2017 by Jenna Miles, ISBN 978-1-4405-9896-8.

Contents

Introduction

Vinyl records are back—in a big way. More and more music lovers are turning to vinyl again for its pure sound, more complete listening experience, and the fun of collecting. No matter your musical tastes, you can find records you'll love to listen to.

Whether you own hundreds of albums or are looking to buy your first one, this book will walk you through everything you need to manage your collection. You'll learn the terminology and lingo associated with record collecting, discover the best ways to build your collection, and find out how to care for and store your vinyl records. While you delve into building or expanding your vinyl collection, you can use the journal pages to jot down important information about each album, thoughts and feelings about the songs on it, and memories related to listening to the record.

I've been in the music business for decades, including running an online radio station, managing an online vinyl retailer and collector community, and overseeing a vinyl-only reissue label. I'll share my expertise and experience to help you gather a musical collection that matches your taste *and* budget.

Listening to the warm, rich sounds of your favorite music on vinyl is a special experience. Recording information about your collection and your memories of listening to it will make this book a keepsake you'll reach for again and again. Get ready to immerse yourself in the high-quality, unique music only vinyl records can provide!

How to Use This Book

This journal will help you keep track of the details of every album you own. In addition to keeping your collection organized, your journal can serve as a musical memoir to pass along with your albums. This book is broken into three parts to help you become the ultimate collector:

- **Part 1: Record Collecting Basics**—Here, you'll learn a brief history of vinyl records, key terms you should know, and where to buy records, both new and used.
- **Part 2: Vinyl Care and Maintenance**—Vinyl records are treasures, and with a bit of care, they can last a lifetime—and more! This section will provide you with all the knowledge an avid collector needs to ensure your collection is maintained and stored in tip-top shape.
- **Part 3: My Vinyl Journal**—This is where you will compose your vinyl story! As you acquire new records, you can keep an index of your finds. The Record Log will allow you to jot down important information to identify which pressing you have and capture any thoughts, feelings, and memories related to that release. There's also space to list your "wants" on your Must-Buy List.

You can personalize this journal however you like—add details of who you listened to the records with, write down your thoughts about different pressings, and give your opinions about cover art or liner notes. You can share it with other vinyl aficionados or keep it just for yourself. There's no wrong way to enjoy your vinyl collection—or this journal.

PART 1

RECORD COLLECTING BASICS

CHAPTER 1

Vinyl Collectors' Terminology

As you start to build your vinyl collection, you'll discover some special terms that you'll need to understand and use in your transactions. This lingo will help you identify exactly what you're buying. Once you familiarize yourself with these terms, you'll be able to converse with other vinyl lovers with ease and confidence.

Parts of a Record

Every record has common parts, as shown in this image. The playable part of a record includes the lead-in groove, which is a blank groove where you place your turntable needle to start the album; the record groove, which is where your turntable needle reads the album's music; and the dead wax/end groove area where the album's recorded tracks end. In the center of the record, you have a center label; this paper-printed area is often used to indicate the side of the record and the track listing on that side of the album. The spindle hole is located in the middle of the center label and is where you attach your album to your turntable.

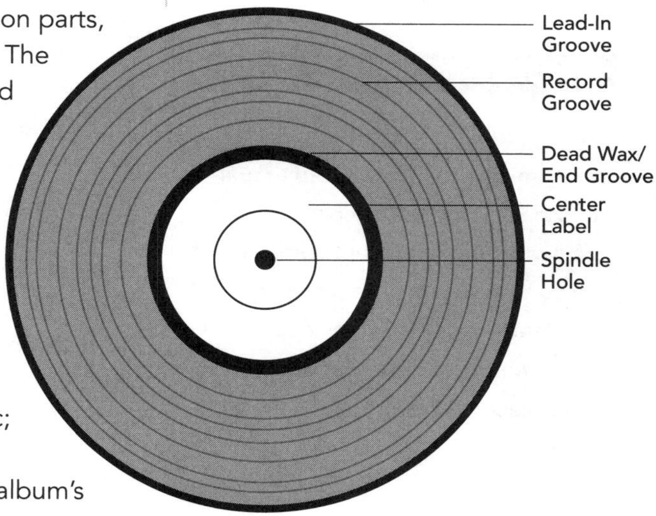

RPMs—Recording Time, Space, and Size

The speed at which a record spins is measured in revolutions per minute (rpm). The total playing time of a record is dependent on the speeds a turntable is able to play and the groove spacing on the disc. Understanding rpm is important because turntables and records are available in different speeds.

A BRIEF HISTORY OF RECORD SPEEDS

The first recordings were produced at varying speeds ranging from 60 rpm to 160 rpm. By 1925, cylinder records began to phase out and 78-rpm shellac disc records became the standard. During this era, both 10-inch records that had a playing time of 3 minutes and 12-inch records that had a 3½- to 5-minute playing time were common. By virtue of the popularity of 10-inch discs during the 78-rpm era, 10-inch discs today are regularly referred to as 78s.

The first 33⅓-rpm "long playing" record was introduced to the market in 1931 by RCA Victor. LPs were pressed on a 30-cm (11.81 inches) disc and had a playing time of about 10 minutes per side. They achieved this by using shallower grooves placed closer together than found on 78-rpm records.

On June 18, 1948, the Columbia Record Company hosted a suspenseful press conference in New York to dazzle everyone with the 33⅓-rpm "microgroove" record, the first album with the ability to play 20 minutes per side. Since the 1950s, the 33⅓-rpm, 12-inch disc is what is commonly released for full-length albums.

RPM Doesn't Equal Record Size

Though most people associate the rpm of a record with an actual record size, diverse record sizes are available in different rpms. For example: 7-inch records are repeatedly referred to as 45s, even though you can get a 7-inch record at 33⅓ rpm.

Recording Times: Speech versus Music

Records can hold more speech than music. Why? The amount and volume of audio affects the size of the groove on an album. When you only have someone talking, you are able to fit more grooves on the record and thus hold more audio.

Vinyl Record Materials

Materials devoted to formulating records have changed and evolved several times over the years. Following are some of the most common materials you'll run into as you purchase records.

SHELLAC

The earliest disc records produced between 1889 and 1894 were made of various materials, including wax and rubber. Shortly after, a shellac-based compound became the standard material. Each manufacturer's exact formula varied, but records were typically made using cardboard and fiber coated with a shellac (wax) resin.

These shellac discs are not known for allowing a quiet, noise-free surface. In fact, shellac records are commonly brittle and require careful treatment. Shellac 78s can break easily, with the remaining pieces loosely connected with the label. They can still be playable if the label holds them together, although there is a recurrent loud "pop" when passing over the crack, which can damage your needle.

PVC

Following World War II, shellac supplies were exceedingly scarce, so records were sometimes pressed on a vinyl composite instead. In the 1950s–1960s, an innovative vinyl composition was broadly introduced. The composition used to fabricate vinyl records has changed and evolved over the years; however, it is primarily a polyvinyl chloride (PVC) blend. This is where the term "vinyl" comes from.

If a record is manufactured with partly recycled vinyl, the quality suffers. For that reason, look for records that are created with virgin vinyl (meaning that they contain no recycled vinyl). During the 1970s energy crisis, substantial petroleum shortages led to records being pressed with recycled vinyl composed of as little as 90 grams of PVC per record. The sound quality of these pressings suffered. Increasing the weight of the vinyl to 160–200 grams has helped avoid warping and damage.

COLORED VINYL

Colored vinyl records have been available since as early as Edison's Amberols, which were a blue-colored shellac cylinder available between 1912 and 1929. Colored discs also appeared during the early 1900s while records were still made of shellac. Early examples include releases from Vocalion, a New York–based record label known for using Edison's vertical-cut method (up until 1916) and their high-quality reddish-brown shellac discs. Between 1916 and 1949, a few other companies offered colored shellac discs, including a blue-shellacked series from Columbia during the 1930s and chocolate-colored pressings from the budget label Perfect Records prior to the 1930s.

In 1949, when RCA Victor launched its 45-rpm format, it began color-coding its records based on genre. For example, pop records were black, country-western were green, and classical were red. RCA discontinued this practice in 1953 because it became too costly to offer these color variations.

Although colored vinyl was occasionally available throughout the 1950s and 1960s, the widespread availability of colored vinyl rebounded in full force during the 1970s. During this time, the album artwork was the primary visual expression of the album, but

The Sound Quality of Colored Vinyl

The color of a record can slightly affect the sound quality. Black records tend to sound best, while many believe that neon, glow-in-the-dark, glitter, and splattered records sound the worst. Black vinyl has the lowest amount of surface noise, followed by standard colors, which do not require any mixing of polyvinyl.

colored discs boosted the artistic value of the entire package. Some colors that were available during the 1970s included clear, transparent white, red, blue, and yellow.

Today, colored vinyl has grown to include almost any possible color variation. Pressing manufacturers like Erika Records in Buena Park, California, can create a record in virtually any custom color. Additionally, they can create colored effects, including splatters, rainbows, swirls, and half-and-half records using just about any color combination.

PICTURE DISCS

Picture discs are records that feature an image visible on the playing area. They began to appear as early as the 1900s—not as discs but as square postcards with miniature records glued on the illustration. Prior to the 1940s, the majority of picture-disc records were made of printed cardboard covered with a thin plastic, which didn't yield the best audio.

Picture discs experienced a resurgence in the 1970s through rereleases, which were used to drive up sales of highly charting albums. Black Sabbath's *Black Sabbath* (1970), Pink Floyd's *Dark Side of the Moon* (1973), and Boston's *Boston* (1976) were among popular albums that featured colorized discs in subsequent releases. *Billboard* magazine credits *To Elvis: Love Still Burning* (1978; a various artist compilation released by Pickwick Records) as the first picture disc to be released in the United States.

FLEXI DISCS

The flexi disc, sometimes referred to as a phonosheet or Soundsheet, is a record made from a flexible vinyl sheet. Flexi discs were introduced in 1962 as an affordable way to include music in printed materials, such as magazines and music books. The use of flexi discs continued throughout the 1970s and 1980s, with diverse and innovative ideas.

One of the more treasured flexi disc releases is The Beatles' Christmas flexi series. Each Christmas from 1963 through 1969, The Beatles sent out flexi discs containing messages and music to their official fan club members. These pressings are popular among Beatles and other vinyl collectors, with complete sets

The McDonald's Flexi Disc

In addition to standard music uses, it also became common for corporations to incorporate flexi discs into their marketing. In 1988, McDonald's held a flexi disc contest that gave one lucky winner a million dollars! Chances of winning were only one in eighty million, but this campaign drew a lot of attention. The disc played the McDonald's "Menu Song," which featured a class of students rapidly learning a full musical narration of their menu. The winning disc was the only copy in which the class successfully sang the track. The winning flexi disc was fortuitously found by thirteen-year-old Scotty Landreth, of Galax, Virginia, piled in a stack of papers he had intended on using to light a fire.

selling for as high as $1,000 and up. Even though flexi disc releases were mainly designed for fun and creative purposes, they are easily worn out, can warp and bend, and were not quality products.

Audiophile Pressing

Although the term "audiophile" can refer to a type of collector, the word is sometimes also used to refer to a specific record pressing. While there is no official standard of an audiophile pressing, the generally accepted definition is a heavy record, mastered with the best available sources and manufactured using quality techniques and careful procedures. Here are a few indicators to determine if a release labeled "audiophile" truly is an audiophile pressing:

- It's pressed on black virgin vinyl. Colored vinyl doesn't always have the same sound quality as black vinyl.
- Detailed mastering information is provided, such as the exact source used and the engineer or studio who mastered it.
- It's pressed on heavyweight 180- to 200-gram vinyl. Although this does not enhance the sound quality, it does help avoid warping.
- It's made with quality audio sources, not sourced from commercial CDs or low-quality digital audio.

Remastered

Large portions of album reissues are often marketed with stickers indicating that they are "remastered." This simply means that the original recording is updated and improved by a mastering engineer and may sound different than previous pressings. Remastering can be a positive attribute of a release, provided a worthy engineer is used and the original source that they master from is of high quality. Within the "remastered" category you might see variations, such as "mastered from original source" or "direct metal mastering."

MASTERED FROM THE ORIGINAL SOURCE

This term means that the music source used is the original recorded source. As an example, say an album was originally released in the 1980s and the master was originally recorded and stored onto a tape. If the album continued being successful, there may be additional master copies that were made, especially digital copies that were created in the digital era. Periodically, record labels will also duplicate from a commercial CD or a low-quality digital file (the same as anyone can purchase anywhere) as their source to save the additional money it costs to acquire the original master.

The original master is usually the highest-quality master available. Therefore, if an album is advertised as "mastered from the original source," you are likely obtaining a high-caliber record, as opposed to ones pressed from CD sources.

DIRECT METAL MASTERING (DMM)

This is the practice of cutting the album audio directly into a metal copper disc instead of the lacquer-coated aluminum disc typically used. Many audiophiles believe that this method creates a better sound. This process removes various stages of plating when manufacturing. It improves noise reduction and pre-echoes, which are faint but audible sounds on an album that you hear slightly before the main recording. Although this technique was once quite popular, it's now scarce because Neumann, the original manufacturer of these lathes, sold the company to Sennheiser and modern lathes and supplies are no longer produced. The lathes that are used today are independently kept and only the engineers who own them know how to use them. There are a few record manufacturers throughout Europe that have DMM facilities. However, it appears as if the art of DMM is no longer present in the United States, as the last company sold its equipment in an auction to the Church of Scientology not long ago. Rumor has it that the Church of Scientology bought up several DMM machines, which they use to transcribe and archive L. Ron Hubbard's speeches.

Matrix Area/Dead Wax

This is the area on a record between the center label and where the grooves end. To aid in identifying the plates used to press the record and the records themselves, if a generic, white center label is used, an alphanumeric code is etched into this dead wax area.

Record Weight

Typically measured in grams, this is the weight of vinyl used to create the record. The standard weight for newly pressed 12-inch LPs is typically between 120 and 150 grams. Records that are more than 150 grams of vinyl are considered "heavyweight" and of higher quality. These typically weigh in at between 180 and 200 grams.

The groove that is carved into the record does not significantly change based on the volume of vinyl used to create the record. Having said that, heavier-weighted vinyl tends to warp less and provides a stable platform for a stylus.

Etching

This is an image that is etched onto an unplayable side of your record. It does not contain audio grooves or music, but instead adds an aesthetically pleasing facet to the record. An etching is commonly made onto single 12-inch EPs that have music on only one side or onto double LPs that contain music on three out of four sides.

Jacket Types

You'll encounter several different types of vinyl jackets as you build your collection. Here are some common variations.

SINGLE JACKET

This is your standard LP jacket that usually holds a single LP. The spine on these jackets can be widened, typically called a wide spine jacket, allowing two LPs to fit inside.

GATEFOLD JACKET

The gatefold jacket is a type of record jacket that contains two panels that are folded in half. It is the same size as a standard LP jacket when closed. This not only provides a canvas for extensive art, but is also typically used to house double LPs. Triple and quad gatefold jackets are also available and are used to house three and four LPs, respectively.

FLIPBACK JACKET

A flipback cover is held together with flaps that fold to the back of the cover from the front, creating a seam.

The Plural of Vinyl Is Not Vinyls...or Is It?

One way to be easily identified as a record buying newbie is to say the word "vinyls." Most record-collecting aficionados insist that you never say *vinyls*, though some people say it's an acceptable term. To be on the safe side, avoid saying *vinyls* when shopping. Instead, when referring to multiple records, call them *vinyl* or *vinyl records*.

Format: 2LP/Double LP, 3LP, 4LP/Quad LP, and More!

Albums are recorded in a variety of lengths. Especially throughout the 1990s and 2000s, artists began recording albums that were lengthier due to the fact that CDs could hold significantly more music than a record. With the resurgence of vinyl, consumers are now demanding releases from the 1990s and 2000s to be pressed to vinyl. The bulk of these albums run longer than 44 minutes (the standard length of a single LP);

therefore, recordings often span across various records encased in one package.

- **Single LP:** This is one 12-inch record. If it is a single, meaning not a full-length album, it will be referred to as a 12-inch EP. If a standard full-length album is on just one record, it is often referred to as an LP.
- **Two records:** A double LP is often indicated by either a 2XLP or 2LP. Commonly found on albums originally released from the 1990s to the present.
- **Three records:** A triple LP is often indicated by either a 3XLP or 3LP. This is commonly used for lengthy soundtracks or a full-length album with accompanying bonus material.
- **More than three records:** You can find any number of records contained in one release, and it will use the same format with the number placed before XLP or LP. For example, Mondo released a limited-edition (1,200 copies) *Batman: The Animated Series* 8XLP box set that contained sixteen full-episode scores on eight 180-gram, 12-inch LPs.

Record Sleeves

Your vinyl should be protected in multiple ways. Protecting the outer jacket as well as the record inside will help preserve the value of your vinyl and keep your collection in good playing condition.

OUTER RECORD SLEEVE

This is a plastic sleeve that is placed over the album. New albums are typically shrink-wrapped, and the sleeve needs to be purchased separately to protect the jacket once the shrink-wrap is removed. These sleeves play a key role in preserving your collection and are further described in Chapter 4.

INNER RECORD SLEEVE

This is the sleeve the record sits in before it is inserted into its jacket. Records are commonly stored in just a plain paper sleeve, but higher-quality records should be stored in a poly-lined sleeve. See further details on sleeves in Chapter 4.

Used Vinyl versus New Vinyl

Now that you know the lingo, should you buy new or used vinyl?

Although millions of records are being pressed each year, not every album is available new…and even if it is, there may be earlier pressings out there that deliver higher-quality sound. Used vinyl tends to be lower in price and more readily available, since many vinyl collectors kept their records in exceptional condition. However, with the vinyl boom in full force, finding stacks of used records is not as common as it was in the early 2010s. The value of used records has increased significantly—if a stockpile of used vinyl is for sale at a reasonably low rate, it is quickly snatched up by professional record buyers who hunt for records daily.

You should select both new and used vinyl with thought and care. Used vinyl is available in all conditions, but there is nothing worse than buying a used record only to find out that it is scratched to pieces and unplayable. Even new vinyl occasionally can be damaged! Once in a while new records are scratched, warped, or the jackets are not in acceptable condition. Or you may find a record that appears immaculate, but when you get home it is troublesome to play.

Purchasing either new or used records is of course acceptable, and most collections contain a combination of both. Do what is suitable for your budget or that particular album. In the next chapter, you will learn more about purchasing new vinyl.

CHAPTER 2

Purchasing New Vinyl

Vinyl sales have increased steadily over the last fifteen-plus years, with records now surpassing CD sales and representing more than 50 percent of the entire physical music market! Newly released vinyl will likely make up a portion of your collection. Whether you visit your local record store, a national chain, or an online store, you can find new vinyl in a wide variety of places nowadays. In this chapter, you'll learn which stores offer vinyl, how to score exclusive releases, and the lowdown on subscription services.

Things to Know When Buying New Vinyl

There are so many places to purchase new vinyl now. After all, more than forty million records were sold in the United States in 2021!

Buying new vinyl is in some ways a simple task, but there are a few tricks you can use to ensure you score the best-quality records and even limited pressings. Following are key things to do when purchasing new vinyl.

EXAMINE THE PACKAGING BEFORE PURCHASING

Records that sit on a retail shelf are often handled several times in the process of reaching a store, then by other customers once they're put out for sale. It is imperative to examine a record to avoid purchasing one with damage. Here's how:

- **Assess the jacket to ensure it is in very good shape.** The amount of acceptable jacket damage is subject to your preference. A slight bend on one of the corners may be okay to some. However, be cautious of significant damage, such as a large crease that may indicate the record has been bent or warped, in turn negatively affecting the playback quality.

- **Check for warping.** Hold the album so you can view the spine head-on and ensure the record itself is straight and does not show any sign of warping. You want to see a flat-looking record package.

BE SURE ONLINE SITES SHIP PROPERLY

There is nothing more heartbreaking than waiting for a record delivery and finding upon arrival that it is packaged in materials clearly not suitable for protecting the record. If purchasing new vinyl online, make sure the sender uses protective mailers. Records are commonly damaged beyond repair during shipping if not properly packaged: They can be warped, the jackets can be destroyed, seams can split, and of course the record could be cracked in half. Luckily, sturdy LP mailers exist, and reputable online sources use them.

BUYING PRE-ORDERS AND BACK-ORDERS

During the 1980s, vinyl record sales began to tank, and the manufacturing of modern pressing machines halted. Even though record sales have surged over the last fifteen-plus years, the production of the equipment to make records has not really evolved. In turn, the demand for vinyl significantly exceeds the worldwide production capacity. That's why, when you are looking to acquire a certain record, you will often be required to either pre-order or back-order an album. Here's the difference:

- **Pre-orders** are when you commit to purchasing an album that has not yet been released. It will be delivered for a future release date.
- A **back-ordered** album is an album that has already been released, but the stock has run out and the retailer is waiting for more copies of the album to arrive.

In both scenarios, you are provided with a date on which you should receive your pre-order or back-order. However, with demand outpacing manufacturing ability, these dates are fluid and it is not uncommon to wait a very long time to get a pre-ordered or back-ordered album.

WORK THROUGH POPS AND SKIPS

When purchasing new vinyl, if issues occur with the way the record sounds, such as pops and skips, but you don't see any scratches, clean your record before attempting to replay it. Don't assume the record is unusable and needs to be returned. At times, even new records collect dust while in the factory. Sometimes residue from the pressing process is left on the record. If the issue is residue on the record from the pressing process, either using a proper cleaning method (see Chapter 5) or playing the record a few times is the best way to get rid of this (the stylus will cut through dust and clean the grooves).

Finding New Vinyl Near and Far

The increase in vinyl popularity means that there are a wide range of outlets where you can purchase new records. In this section, you will find examples of all the different types of places to score new vinyl, from your local independent option to large national outlets to online stores.

Even with the variety of places to buy records nowadays, it is occasionally difficult to secure copies of new releases and reissues. That's why you'll also find a collection of tips on how to score the scarcer and limited-availability albums you might want to add to your collection.

> **Stay In the Know**
>
> **The best way to keep up to date on new releases and limited pressings is to join the Vinyl Collective community (www.vinylcollective.com)! With over thirty thousand like-minded vinyl addicts, you will be sure to hear about upcoming vinyl pressings here first.**

Independent Record Stores

The independent, or indie, record store is an independently owned, local brick-and-mortar record store that is not affiliated with a national chain. Over the last fifteen years, major music retail chains have dwindled and gone out of business, while the number of independently owned record stores has grown. Independent stores are more of a community rather than just a regular retail store. Frequently, indie stores are closely connected with artists and labels, providing relationships that are rewarding for the consumer.

Indie retail store staff often have the same passion for music as their customers. A really good indie store will know their regular customers and will work with you to get the records you need. Build a relationship with your indie store, because they will be happy to help you collect both the basics and the difficult to find rarities.

The Decline of Major Music Retailers

The early 2000s was a tough time for music, notably for physical media. The Internet made digital music pirating effortless, which contributed significantly to dwindling sales. As a result of that and other factors, most music retailers went out of business in that time period. Only a few music-focused retail chains still exist, including FYE in the United States, Sunrise Records in Canada, and HMV in the United Kingdom.

Chain Retailers Selling Vinyl

The majority of chain retailers that currently sell vinyl are not music specific and include companies that might surprise you with their vinyl selection, including Whole Foods and Cracker Barrel! Here are worthwhile retailers to hit up for vinyl.

URBAN OUTFITTERS

Clothing retailer Urban Outfitters currently stocks a fairly generous selection of vinyl. They carry a mixture of both new releases and reissues spanning a range of genres such as classic rock, indie, hip-hop, rock, and more. They also offer a commendable array of titles in colors exclusively available through their stores.

BARNES & NOBLE

Best known for its book sales, Barnes & Noble is now also an excellent source for new records. Their record section is set up similarly to what you used to experience within traditional music retail stores, and they offer a diverse selection of vinyl spanning a variety of genres.

FYE

Entertainment and pop culture retailer FYE (For Your Entertainment) sells vinyl both online and in brick-and-mortar shops in malls throughout the United States. FYE carries an extensive selection of new vinyl, alongside a wide variety of exclusive colored pressings only available through them.

NEWBURY COMICS

Both a music and comic book retailer, Newbury Comics is a great source for vinyl, particularly for limited vinyl sold only through them. They currently stock a huge selection of records on color variants available only at their retail stores and on their website. Cherished Newbury exclusives include:

- Lorde's *Pure Heroine* vinyl on a clear variant, limited to fifteen hundred copies.
- No Doubt's *Tragic Kingdom* multicolor marble colored vinyl, limited to eight hundred copies.
- Interpol's *Turn on the Bright Lights* on red and black splatter vinyl, limited to seven hundred and fifty copies.

Each of these titles is out of print and has a resale value of over $500.

Check the Album Before Purchasing

Use extra caution and carefully examine records when shopping at large retailers, as their process for handling and displaying vinyl often differs from an independent record store's. Indie record store owners are almost always record collectors themselves and therefore put thorough care and attention into maintaining the quality of records they put on their shelves.

WHOLE FOODS, CRACKER BARREL, AND MORE

As vinyl rebounded, a few unexpected retailers began stocking vinyl. In 2013, Whole Foods launched a vinyl record section alongside its sale of organic vegetables. In the United Kingdom, several retail chains tried out the sale of records alongside their other products, such as Gap and grocery stores Tesco and Aldi. In early 2016, the US restaurant chain Cracker Barrel entered the vinyl market with an exclusive numbered release of Joey + Rory's *Hymns That Are Important to Us*. Other major stores such as Walmart and Target now also regularly stock a selection of records.

Online Retailers

Online stores are one of the most popular ways to obtain new vinyl. Prior to the vinyl rebound, a considerable number of major brick-and-mortar retailers were hesitant to stock vinyl and primarily sold CDs. Online was a way to offer vinyl to the market without large investments in stock and shelf space. A generous fraction of vinyl released prior to the revival was done through do-it-yourself niche sites, the artist directly, and Amazon. Today, the market has changed somewhat but still heavily features Amazon.

AMAZON

Amazon (www.amazon.com) is the single largest retailer of vinyl, with approximately 40 percent of the market share as of 2021. Purchasing vinyl from Amazon is a straightforward retail process. They offer free two-day shipping on some albums for Amazon Prime members, have the largest selection available, and often carry quite a bit of stock.

Amazon also allows others to sell through their site, similar to eBay and Discogs, so it can also be used as a way to obtain out-of-print, new, and used vinyl through third-party sellers.

ARTIST EXCLUSIVES

Buying direct from a musician is typically the best way to support them, as they often receive the largest royalty portion from selling directly to the customer. To encourage this, artists now sell exclusive vinyl variants directly to

> **Exclusives in Special Colors**
>
> With the popularity of vinyl releases and reissues, countless titles are being pressed on multiple color variants available exclusively through certain retailers, and frequently through the artists' websites directly. If you hear about a current record in a particular color, be sure to verify where this item is available before heading out to just any record shop.

their fans from their websites or on their tours. A lot of artists also offer vinyl new releases or album reissues directly through their own websites. When scoping out a new release, it is always wise to check the artist's website to see if they will be offering a limited color, autographed copies, or additional bonus items that you can purchase directly through them.

INDEPENDENT ONLINE RETAILERS

Equivalent to the indie brick-and-mortar retailers, several independent vinyl web stores exist. Here are a few of the major online vinyl retailers that are reliable and excellent to shop from.

ACOUSTIC SOUNDS

Acoustic Sounds (www.acousticsounds.com) is an online business that specializes in the sale of audiophile vinyl, super audio CDs (SACDs), DVD-audio, and high-quality equipment. Launched in 1986, Acoustic Sounds started off as a mail-order business from the founder's (Chad Kassem) apartment and has grown into one of the largest online suppliers of vinyl, specifically audiophile and collectible records.

In 2011, Acoustic Sounds launched their own pressing plant, Quality Record Pressings (QRP), allowing them to further control and improve the quality of their releases. The Acoustic Sounds website currently has a large selection of reissues exclusively released by them in addition to audiophile records from other labels. The website also has a "vault" section that includes rare and valuable records.

SRC VINYL

The store I currently own, SRC Vinyl (www.srcvinyl.com), is a one-stop shop for new, unopened vinyl that ships from both Canada and the United States. My spouse, Danny Keyes, and I inadvertently started SRC Vinyl in 2006 when our already struggling business, an online radio station called Punk Radio Cast, was thrown under by the recession. A record label–owning friend of ours suggested that we might stay in business for a few months if we traded ads in exchange for CDs and records. Punk Radio Cast had a large audience who were passionate about music; therefore, selling product was fairly simple.

By 2012, we became acquainted with what record collectors wanted and as a result developed relationships with a variety of record labels and began reissuing records that were in demand but not available on vinyl. SRC Vinyl exists today as a vinyl-centric online store with a catalog of more than five thousand new vinyl records available at any given time, including a large selection of exclusive titles and color variants.

Vinyl Subscription Services

These types of music services have been around since 1955, when Columbia Records launched its Columbia Record Club, later renamed Columbia House. Columbia House sold music to consumers through direct mail, and all titles made available through the subscription were at least six months old. The service was launched to provide consumers living in rural areas who did not have access to brick-and-mortar stores a way to purchase albums. Columbia House continued to operate as a music subscription service up until 2009. While it has been rumored that Columbia House would relaunch as a vinyl subscription service, that has yet to happen.

A handful of records, many that have gone on to sell for quite high prices, were originally available through vinyl subscriptions and fan clubs. Sub Pop Records launched a singles club that featured 7-inch singles. The first set was issued from November 1988 to December 1993, the second between April 1998 and March

2002, and the third between August 2008 and October 2009. The debut single was Nirvana's "Love Buzz b/w Big Cheese." This 7-inch single was limited to one thousand copies and has a median selling price of over $4,000, with one copy selling for over $7,000 on the Discogs website.

THIRD MAN RECORDS

Third Man Records, the record label of Jack White of The White Stripes, has had its popular Vault subscription service since 2009. Each quarter, subscribers receive an exclusive Vault LP, a Vault 7-inch, and a bonus item that has included T-shirts, posters, postcards, and DVDs. The first Vault package was a mono version of The White Stripes album *Icky Thump*, which has sold for as high as $689. Subscriptions can include extra perks like a discount at the Third Man Records store and a discount on a subscription to the Tidal music streaming service.

VINYL ME, PLEASE

Another vinyl subscription service, Vinyl Me, Please (www.vinylmeplease.com), sends subscribers a new or reissued exclusive album every month. Subscribers can choose one record each month from a small selection of three or four titles, which are almost always colored vinyl.

VNYL

The subscription service VNYL (www.vnyl.org) sends their subscribers a monthly shipment of 1–3 records, curated specifically for them based on information provided. Subscriptions are priced based on the number of records you receive per month and the length of your subscription.

Bootleg Records

A bootleg or unofficial record is an album that is not officially released by the artist or record label. Bootleg records can consist of either an illegally duplicated album or an illegally recorded live performance that is sold and circulated on vinyl. Although bootleggers financially profit from the sale of these records, the label and the artist never earn a dime. One way the industry combats bootlegs is by immediately releasing the same album officially. If the official version was produced with improved quality, this would decrease the demand for the bootleg and would essentially cease the production of the bootleg.

Bootlegs are no longer produced in the numbers that they once were, so don't worry too much about a newly manufactured product being a bootleg. With the scarcity of record pressing machines, there is not enough equipment available to produce bootlegs. However, with older titles, bootleg versions are likely to exist. If you are ever unsure if an album you are interested in is a bootleg, here are a few ways to verify:

- Check that the record is shrink-wrapped and sealed. Bootlegs rarely have that level of production.
- Check the album for a catalog number, logos from the record label, and legal copy indicating who released and distributed it. Bootleggers do not include this detailed information.
- Check Discogs; they list if a pressing is official or not.
- If purchasing on eBay, make sure the seller shows pictures of the item before buying.

Don't be afraid if you are in doubt to confirm with the seller that it is not a bootleg.

Record Store Day

Record Store Day is the largest record collectors event of the year. The first Record Store Day was April 19, 2008, and it continues to occur annually on the third Saturday of April. This day is a celebration of the record store, the customer, and most importantly the musicians who make this music available. Just about every record store across North America and countless worldwide offer a giant celebration on this day, which includes official Record Store Day releases, sales, live performances, and other events organized by the record store.

A Record Store Day committee works with various independent and major labels to designate several titles that are sanctioned as official Record Store Day titles and only available through participating stores worldwide. These titles are limited and desired by record collectors to the extent that many begin lining up hours or even days prior to the store opening!

Record Store Day releases are always limited in quantity, and a hefty portion sell out in stores within the first hour. If you are in search of a record, or several records, on the list, you have to head out to your local record shop early that day.

More on Record Store Day

Check out www.recordstoreday.com for information on upcoming events, participating stores, and releases related to Record Store Day.

CHAPTER 3

Purchasing Used Vinyl

The best way to start building a collection is by acquiring a few reasonably priced used records. New records typically cost between $15 and $60, whereas you can buy tons of used records for under $15. Purchasing a few used records that are on the lower end of the price spectrum will help you get comfortable operating a turntable and learning how to handle records before you invest more money in the hobby.

Things to Know When Buying Used Vinyl

Even the act of buying used records is a skill in itself. You usually can't test the records before you buy them, and used records are commonly not returnable.

When buying used records, you will probably have to sort through a ton of junk before choosing a quality record. No matter where you sift through used records, whether it be garage sales, thrift shops, or record stores, take your time. Don't be afraid to grab a bunch of records and move aside to examine them individually, choosing only the ones that are in a satisfying condition. Not all records need to be in pristine, mint condition, but you need time to be sure you buy vinyl with a lot of life left in it.

You can build a large collection of vinyl on a budget by purchasing used. However, a considerable amount of used vinyl is junk and not worth any money. Focus on figuring out the condition of a record first, and then weigh any damage against the cost of the record. A record may have a few of the issues mentioned in this chapter, but at the right price it may still be worth it. For example, there is nothing wrong with buying a record for a dollar that has a beat-up jacket if your only intentions are to play it and not resell it.

Now let's review how to inspect used records to ensure you come home with quality finds.

Examine the Packaging

The first component to examine is the jacket's condition. Here are the issues you may encounter:

- **Water damage:** If there is water damage on the record jacket, the actual record may have been exposed to water too. Vinyl with minimal water damage can usually still be used once properly cleaned. However, avoid records that smell musty or moldy.
- **Jacket wear and tear:** Examine the jacket for various types of wear and tear. Heavily used or improperly stored records will have significant damage to the jacket, such as seam splits, a split on the edge of the jacket, or ring wear (a circular ring from the record itself that shows up on the jacket when records are stored incorrectly).
- **Missing inner sleeve:** When properly stored, vinyl records are supposed to sit in an inner sleeve. It doesn't matter as much what type of sleeve as long as there is one. If there is no inner sleeve, the record was not stored properly and you'll need to carefully inspect the record for damage.
- **Missing inserts:** If you are considering purchasing a specific release, such as Alice Cooper's *School's Out*, which included a report card with track listings as an insert and a pair of paper panties, you should be sure these components are in the used version. An easy way to get all the information on the contents of a specific pressing is to search a title on Discogs (www.discogs.com), a comprehensive music database.
- **Markings on the jacket:** This is especially common among used records. Record stores used to place a sticker directly on the jacket or even just wrote the price directly on the cover. People also sometimes wrote their names on their records to know whose was whose. These markings do not diminish sound quality, of course, but are a personal preference to take into account when purchasing. Unless your goal is to buy and resell the record (aka, flipping the record), you may not be concerned too much with minor jacket wear and

tear and other damage such as markings on the jacket. If you are aiming to land a good-quality record to listen to, simply ensure that none of these markings on the jacket indicate potential heavy usage or damage to the actual record itself.

Examine the Record

It is tough to distinguish whether a record has been played on proper equipment and carefully handled, but here are some tips so you can do the best job possible. First, try to examine the record in a brightly lit area, preferably using a high-lumen desk lamp or natural sunlight. You can also invest in a miniature magnifying glass with a tiny but bright light for as little as $10. If you spin the record around while in a brightly lit area, the light will reflect off the record, enabling you to identify scratches, scuffs, or other damage. Following are the main issues you should watch for.

CORRECT RECORD

First and foremost, make sure that the record in the jacket is in fact the correct record. If the album jacket is a gatefold and there is only one record, refer to the center label to verify if a second LP should have been included. You could also check on Discogs to verify if there should be two LPs.

SCUFFS

Scuffs are usually caused by records rubbing up against something else because they were not properly stored in protective sleeves. Depending on how thick the groove is cut and the weight of the vinyl, these scuffs may affect the way the record plays.

SCRATCHES

Similar to scuffs, light scratches do not interfere with the sound playback, while deeper scratches

Assessing How Bad the Damage Is

If you find any scratches, scuffs, groove wear, or needle drop damage, touch them delicately with your finger to determine how deep the damage is. A seemingly light scuff could turn out to be a deep scratch, which you'll want to avoid.

will yield a dreadful spinning experience. Scratches that appear in the direction of the groove rather than across it are known as tramlines. These types of scratches are tougher to spot but can cause a needle to stick, permanently repeating the groove.

GROOVE WEAR

Visual indications of possible extensive groove wear include a white lining within the groove or a hazy grayish-colored groove. A heavy tracking arm or using a worn-out stylus typically causes groove wear. Groove wear can be difficult to visually detect, but you will hear a distortion in the sound if you're able to play the record.

NEEDLE DROP DAMAGE

This occurs when a needle is dropped too heavily onto a record, and can cause a scratch or tiny divot. The start of the first track on all sides (where a needle is typically dropped to start the record) is where damage is likely to occur. This damage can cause clicks and pops. Carefully examine the lead-in groove on both sides of the record to locate signs of needle drop damage.

CENTER LABEL AND SPINDLE HOLE

The spindle hole can indicate how often the record was played. Marks around the hole indicate heavy use. If the spindle hole is misshaped, that will also signify previous record owners played the record often. Scratches on the center label may indicate the previous user often bumped the spindle into the record itself.

WARPED DISC

Heavy warping of a record can indicate possible exposure to heat or that the record was stored improperly (likely flat as opposed to vertically).

Identifying the Pressing Version

When searching for a particular album, you will almost always encounter different pressing versions of a release. There is always an original release for every record release, meaning the first batch of records pressed for a specific album, and reissues, which refer to any subsequent pressings for an album. With vinyl pressed

Which Pressing Is It?

Previously, the act of figuring out which version of an album you have was a daunting research task. However, now you can quickly look up key data (like the catalog number or barcode) on Discogs (www.discogs.com), the largest online music database, to determine a record version easily and effortlessly.

in limited quantities, almost all releases have one original pressing and several reissues.

While each record label has a different way of classifying and cataloging its releases, a set of identifiers can help you distinguish which pressing it is. To identify a record, you'll first collect the following data, then use it to establish a pressing version.

EXAMINE THE JACKET AND INSERT

Locate and take note of the information on an album jacket:

- **Catalog number:** Typically, a combination of letters and numbers is assigned to the album by the record label. The catalog number is often listed on the spine and sometimes in small print on the back of the album.
- **Record label:** The label's name is located on the spine or back of the album. The record label may vary by country of release or if an album moves to a different record label.
- **Country and year released:** This information is usually found on the back of the album at the very bottom in small print. Frequently, even if released at the same time, a release can vary from country to country. It may have different tracks or was pressed at a different location. Releases can even vary in pressing quality.
- **Barcode:** Barcodes and UPCs are unique codes placed on the record that can help determine the version. Although barcodes are very handy at helping to differentiate a version quickly, they did not become commonly used on records until the mid-1980s.
- **Artwork:** Different versions of an album can include a

different insert or cover artwork. Some albums may come with a "hype sticker" placed on the shrink-wrap or jacket itself that could help indicate which version it is.

EXAMINE THE RECORD

Once you have noted all the relevant information on the jacket, you should next inspect the following on the record itself:

- **Center label:** A pressing may have a center label design that is unique to it. Or a variety of the information mentioned previously can be located on the center label, such as catalog number, record label, country, and year released.
- **Matrix number:** The matrix number is an identifying code inscribed on the dead wax area near the center label. This code can be unique to the pressing and may help pinpoint it.
- **Appearance of the record:** Sometimes, recognizing a version is as simple as looking at the record itself and determining the color of the wax or any other unique feature such as an etching.

Grading Used Records

Used record sellers, such as record shops and thrift and antique stores, will often grade records. Grading records allows the seller to obtain a higher price for it while indicating the record's condition to the buyer. If you come across records that are graded, they are likely graded using the Goldmine Grading Guide. You can mark these grades in the journal portion of this book to note your collection's status. Following is a breakdown of each grade in the system along with its abbreviation, but for even more extensive information on record grading and the value of records, check out the Goldmine website at www.goldminemag.com.

STILL SEALED (SS)

An SS grade indicates that the record is still sealed and implies that it has never been played. Be wary, though—unscrupulous retailers sometimes just reseal records if they have the equipment to do so. Although it is almost impossible to be 100 percent certain the record was not resealed by a retailer, there are some indicators that may help you decide if it is truly in SS condition. Inspect the record to see if you notice any wear on the jacket, such as tears or scuffs on the paper. Additionally, if the record is still sealed and several years old, it likely could include an original retail pricing or promotional sticker. These records are priced at the highest value.

MINT (M)

Records graded as Mint may have never been played and may still be sealed. They must be in perfect condition in every way. These records are priced at the highest value.

NEAR MINT (NM OR M–)

A Near Mint record is nearly untouched and shows no sign of wear and tear. The LP cover should have no creases, seam splits, or other defects. All components should be included and should be in pristine condition.

VERY GOOD PLUS (VG+)

VG+ records will show minimal sign of handling and/or use. However, it should be apparent that the owner took excellent care of the record. These are generally worth approximately 50 percent of the Near Mint value. The record surface may have minimal signs of wear, such as a slight warp or scuff or scratches that do not affect the play. Jackets may have a bit of ring wear or slight discoloration, but it should be barely noticeable. The spindle hole should not be misshaped (that happens with heavy play).

VERY GOOD (VG)

Generally worth around 25 percent of the Near Mint value, VG records will show heavier signs of usage. Groove wear will also become noticeable. The scratches and scuffs may be faintly apparent when listening to the record. There may be writing or stickers on the jacket.

GOOD (G) OR GOOD PLUS (G+)

Records graded Good or Good Plus are worth approximately 10–15 percent of the Near Mint value. These records still may play well without skipping, but they will have surface noises, scratches, and visible groove wear. The jacket will have seam splits, ring wear, writing, or other damage.

POOR (P) OR FAIR (F)

Poor or Fair records are typically worth 0–5 percent of the Near

Why Do I See Two Grades?

You might come across a record with two grades—one for the record itself and one for the jacket. The jacket may be damaged with a Poor (P) rating, but the record is in Very Good (VG) condition. If it is an album you want to play but don't necessarily care about the jacket, you could consider buying a generic replacement sleeve.

Mint value. The record can be challenging to play, with frequent skipping or repeating. The vinyl is often crudely warped or cracked. Jackets can be water damaged, heavily damaged, or even missing. An album with a Fair grade should still be playable with some defects, whereas an album with a Poor grade may have significantly more defects.

Where to Buy Used Vinyl In Person

A thrilling aspect of collecting is the process of digging for the records to add to your collection. Often, used records are the only way to acquire certain titles because they may be out of print, meaning no current copies are being produced. Just as with new vinyl, you can find used records in stores near your home or online. Following are some stops you might want to make on your journey to build your vinyl collection.

LOCAL RECORD SHOPS

Experienced used record collectors shop often, some weekly, and others (remarkably) almost daily! Good records don't stay on the shelf for a long time, so frequent visits to your local record shop will increase your likelihood of finding gems.

Spending a good amount of time at the local record store will also enable you to build relationships with the staff. They are likely avid record collectors and can help you find the records you want. At a quality local record store, you should feel comfortable spending a lot of time there and feel at ease asking questions.

GARAGE AND ESTATE SALES

Shopping at garage and estate sales is a great way to add to your record collection—if you know how to approach them. Here are tips for shopping at both estate and garage sales:

1. **Generate a plan:** If you're planning multiple stops, make a plan before you leave the house. The website www.estatesales.net lists upcoming estate sales throughout the United States. Garage sale listings can be found on websites such as Craigslist and Nextdoor, Kijiji (in Canada), and on local Facebook forums. In some instances, these listings can indicate what categories of vinyl they will be selling, allowing you to prioritize which ones to hit up first, based on your interests.
2. **Set a budget and bring cash:** Garage and estate sales are almost always cash only. Setting a budget beforehand will help you avoid purchasing unnecessary stuff. That said, consider bringing additional cash just in case you find an amazing rarity. Infrequently, garage and estate sales accept credit or debit cards…but even if they do, cash is always better if you are negotiating.
3. **Inspect the records:** Using the methods mentioned earlier in this chapter, inspect the records to determine if the conditions of the records are acceptable before you decide what you are willing to pay.
4. **Negotiate:** Records at garage and estate sales should be significantly cheaper than those at a local record shop. Don't be afraid to politely request a lower price than the one indicated.
5. **Consider buying a large quantity:** Remember, the goal of estate and garage sales is to get rid of as much stuff as possible. Therefore, you might be able to score an exceptional deal if you offer to buy a bunch of records instead of just one or two. If you buy a large quantity of records, but only want to keep a few titles, your local record shop may be inclined to purchase the remainder. This is an excellent strategy when the seller is motivated to sell all the records, versus the few you may be interested in. You can also try this method if you

are at a busy garage sale and do not have time to rummage through the records before others grab up records you haven't had a chance to look at.

THRIFT AND ANTIQUE STORES

With the increase of vinyl sales, thrift and antique stores are starting to individually grade and price records higher than ever, especially within metropolitan areas, so be cautious. Chain thrift stores are also starting to recognize the demand for vinyl and have increased their prices. That doesn't necessarily imply that you'll never find a good deal at one of these spots, however. In fact, many antique dealers focus on items that have higher price points and may not pay too much attention to pricing their vinyl.

An excellent thrift and antique shopping strategy is to visit often and to earn the friendship of the dealers. Avid record collectors visit the chain thrift stores with donation boxes almost daily! Because antique shops usually do not accept donations, they tend to obtain stock less often, and a weekly or biweekly visit may be sufficient. Once again, becoming friends with the thrift and antique dealers will provide an advantage, and they can likely provide an idea as to how often they bring in stock.

RECORD SHOWS

Record shows are events where groups of record vendors come together in various cities across the world to sell vinyl. Record shows were quite popular among collectors before the current vinyl boom happened. Not too long ago, there was a shortage of retail outlets to purchase vinyl. Chain retailers were not selling records and there weren't nearly as many independent record stores around, either. These shows brought together nearby vendors to

A Deal but Not a Steal

Clever antique and thrift store owners will now look online for pricing guidelines before putting vinyl out for sale. Even charitable thrift stores realize they should glance online for the value of a record before placing it out for sale, so it's harder than ever to find a gem for a steal.

provide record collectors a chance to do some extensive shopping.

While select vendors sell new records, a large number of them sell older, used vinyl. Record shows usually occur in hotels, churches, schools, and other temporary rented facilities. Although the majority of products for sale at these shows are records, often other vendors with unique music-related products and memorabilia are included. These events are also a way to connect with other vinyl collectors within your area. They are a truly enjoyable and unique experience.

Record shows usually charge a nominal entrance fee. To find out about record shows in your area, visit your local record shop and ask about any upcoming events.

Purchasing Used Vinyl Online

There are quite a few ways to purchase used vinyl on the Internet. Here are a few spots that collectors find reputable.

DISCOGS

Discogs is not just a website; it is the world's largest music database and marketplace with more than 7.1 million titles listed. The content within the Discogs database is completely user generated and is updated constantly. Discogs is an excellent tool to use while hunting for used records to verify both a pressing version and the current market value of a record. Discogs provides a pricing scale that accumulates the history of sales for every item on the site and highlights the lowest price, the median (average), and the highest price each item has ever sold for. This information gives you a clear indication as to what a record is worth. Additionally, if you download the free Discogs app, you can use your cell phone camera to scan the barcode on the record jacket and instantly locate the item within the Discogs marketplace. If a barcode is not available, you can enter the catalog number into Discogs to directly link to the item.

Discogs is also a marketplace that connects buyers with sellers from all over the world, to facilitate shopping for both discount and rare records. Records on Discogs are graded using the Goldmine Grading Guide. Buyers also rate their experience with sellers, allowing you to easily pinpoint how reputable they are. A seller's location is provided so you can estimate shipping properly. All payments for Discogs sales are made through PayPal, and the seller has to provide PayPal with tracking information for your package. PayPal employs a buyer-supportive return policy, and it is likely if something goes wrong they will assist you. PayPal also offers a 180-day dispute time frame in case the records are not received.

EBAY

Comparable to Discogs, eBay provides a consumer-to-consumer sales forum. However, on eBay you are bidding on the records, whereas Discogs sellers list a set price. eBay is primarily utilized to sell valuable records as opposed to less expensive albums. eBay is also a good spot to find larger collections at a discount price. eBay does not provide a pricing guideline or history for the sale of its items directly, but you can visit Popsike (www.popsike.com) to view sales history on a specific item. If you type an album title into Popsike, it will show the various sales that have occurred for that specific item, including the prices they were sold at and the dates they were sold. This tool ensures that you are paying a fair price for records on eBay.

Similar to Discogs, eBay does not directly sell items. The sellers are rated by the buyers and vice versa, and sellers can provide feedback in regard to their experience. eBay offers a way to initiate a dispute with a seller if an issue arises. Using PayPal for all your eBay purchases will also ensure protection.

ONLINE MARKETPLACES

Those who decide to no longer collect vinyl or those who have inherited a collection of records they don't want often advertise records locally through online classified ads. Two magnificent online sources to locate used vinyl in your area are the local listings on Craigslist (www.craigslist.org) in the United States and Kijiji (www.kijiji.ca) in Canada. Amazon also offers used vinyl listings for just about every album currently available.

PART 2

VINYL CARE AND MAINTENANCE

CHAPTER 4

Storing Records

Storing records requires a bit of thought and care. This chapter covers everything you need to know to handle and store your vinyl so that your records are protected. You'll also get advice on insuring your collection—something people often don't realize they can do until it's too late.

How to Properly Handle a Record

One of the best ways to preserve your collection is to make sure you are carefully handling and storing your records. Here's the procedure you should use to remove a record from a jacket and how to place it back into the jacket properly:

1. Don't have food or drink nearby.
2. Wash your hands before handling records or wear a pair of clean, lint-free white gloves.
3. To remove a record from the jacket, open the jacket and carefully pull out the record's inner sleeve.
4. To extract the record from the inner sleeve, open the inner sleeve and let the record slide into an open hand. When it touches your hand, the edge of the record should touch your thumb, and you should be able to handle the center label with your middle finger. Avoid touching the grooved area of the actual record itself if possible.

Storing a Record after You Play It

Likewise, storing an album back in its case after you play it is also important. Here's how to do it:

1. Before storing your album, clean it (using one of the methods discussed in Chapter 5) to ensure no dust or dirt remains on the record.

2. To avoid scratches and dust accumulation, always store your album in its inner sleeve. Place the record back in by bowing open the inner sleeve and carefully sliding it back in. Never drop a record into the inner sleeve. Remember to wash your hands before handling the record.
3. Place the album jacket into the plastic outer sleeve.
4. How you store your records will be different than the way they are stored when you purchase them. Place the record housed in its inner sleeve behind the album jacket, between the jacket and the outer sleeve. Storing your vinyl in its inner sleeve only, outside the jacket, will guarantee you do not seam split your jacket and prevents ring wear, increasing the likelihood of keeping both the album and jacket in a pristine condition.

Proper Methods for Storing Your Collection

One of the most common ways records become damaged is improper storage or mishandling. Here are fundamental points to remember when choosing how and where to store your records.

AVOID DIRECT SUNLIGHT AND HEAT

Records are best kept at or below room temperature away from direct sunlight. One reason is because UV rays can cause discoloring of the record jacket. Additionally, records themselves are susceptible to intense heat. With exposure to extremely hot, direct sunlight, records can warp and even melt!

If you purchase vinyl online, consider ways to avoid possible heat exposure during delivery. If you are not home when a package is delivered, the carrier will often place your package outside anywhere that is convenient. During the hot months, I ensure my records are delivered to my workplace, or I leave a note for the carrier to place the records in a specific place away from direct sunlight.

AVOID EXTREME COLD

Moderate coolness does not cause damage to records, but

extreme cold (below freezing point) can cause records to warp if they are not stored correctly or are brought back to room temperature too quickly. If you ever move vinyl from a very cool temperature to room temperature, be sure to allow them to acclimatize before handling to avoid warping.

DO NOT STACK RECORDS

Store your albums in an upright, completely vertical position and never lay them flat or on top of each other. Do not store them upright on an angle either; that placement can also warp the record. There are various options for keeping your records in an upright position (more on that later in this chapter).

STORE IN A RELATIVELY DRY AREA

Be sure to keep your records in a room that has a relative humidity of 35–40 percent. Storing them in a basement—especially a wet or musty basement—can harm the records. You should also avoid attics, garages, or sheds because they tend to be quite moist. Moisture is damaging to both the record jacket and vinyl.

Additionally, if a room is too dry, the record jackets can become brittle, and the vinyl can get damaged. If you are limited to an area that is too moist or dry, you can invest in a humidifier or dehumidifier to control the amount of moisture in the room.

Record Sleeves

To properly store a record and maintain the best condition possible, you need both an inner sleeve to protect the album itself and an outer sleeve to preserve the record jacket. There are several different inner and outer sleeves available on the market. Let's explore the available types so you can purchase what's right for you.

INNER SLEEVES

These are the sleeves you place over the record. Proper inner sleeves protect the actual LPs from dust and dirt while also preventing them from getting scratched. Here are the different types and their pros and cons:

PAPER SLEEVES

Standard paper inner sleeves that records are typically housed in are considered low quality and can deteriorate the wax. Paper sleeves are cost-effective, but they provide the least amount of protection. Although they cover the record and protect it from dirt and dust, paper can scratch the album. If you elect to use paper sleeves, ensure they are at a minimum acid-free.

POLYETHYLENE

Polyethylene sleeves are soft and the least damaging to records. They are available in either a low-density version created from low-static polyethylene or a high-density version made from pure antistatic polyethylene. Due to their soft properties, they will not scratch your records or introduce static, keeping your records in tip-top shape.

One issue with these sleeves is that the plastic is flimsy, causing them to bunch up when inside your record jacket. Unlike the typical square shapes, round bottom versions are available that reduce the bunching effect.

ACID-FREE POLY-LINED

This is a paper sleeve with a polyethylene lining inside. They provide the identical sturdiness as paper sleeves, but the soft, smooth polyethylene lining on the inside prevents the scratching that paper can cause.

PAPER-LINED POLY (RICE PAPER SLEEVE)

Paper-lined polyethylene sleeves are often referred to by a few names, including high-density polyethylene sleeves, HDPE sleeves, or rice paper sleeves. This is the sleeve I recommend. The quality of these sleeves is similar to polyethylene sleeves, except they consist of three layers of high-density, antistatic polyethylene and a single sheet of acid-free paper. The acid-free paper enables the sleeve to be sturdy and eliminates the bunching issue. The acid-free paper is sandwiched between two of the three layers of polyethylene, making sure that the paper never comes into direct contact with the record.

OUTER SLEEVES

Outer sleeves are made of plastic, typically polyethylene, polypropylene, polyvinyl, or polyester. They are available in a variety of thicknesses, measured in mils. Outer sleeves are placed over your jacket to protect your records from dust and dirt.

POLYPROPYLENE SLEEVES

These reasonably priced sleeves are significantly thinner and crystal clear compared to polyethylene sleeves. Because they are thin, they tend to rip quite easily, making them best suited for shorter-term storage. They have a clear and shiny appearance, making them most useful for displaying record covers.

POLYETHYLENE SLEEVES

These are the most commonly used and recommended sleeves. Polyethylene sleeves are made in all album sizes, with thickness options typically varying from 2.5 to 6 mils. The greater the thickness, the sturdier the sleeves are and the longer they last. Experienced collectors most commonly use the 3-mil polyethylene sleeves. These are available with either an opening at the top or a resealable flap. If you can confirm the polyethylene sleeves are produced using 100 percent virgin polyethylene, they will not yellow or crack over time. These sleeves are best suited for the long-term preservation of your collection.

POLYVINYL

Polyvinyl sleeves are incredibly thick and durable. These sleeves are best for short-term storage as the sleeves can stick to the cover of the jacket, ruining the cover art if exposed to heat or used over an extensive period.

POLYESTER SLEEVES

Polyester sleeves, also called Mylar sleeves, are durable and

Where to Buy Record Sleeves

Record inner and outer sleeves can be purchased at independent record stores or online at the indie record stores mentioned, Acoustic Sounds and SRC Vinyl. If you are considering purchasing larger quantities of sleeves, in excess of a few hundred, an excellent source is Bags Unlimited (www.bagsunlimited.com), an online retailer from Rochester, New York, that offers protection supplies of all sorts.

crystal clear. These sleeves are the only sleeve recognized by the Library of Congress for archiving vinyl records. These are the ultimate sleeve for preserving and protecting your collection, but they are significantly more expensive than other sleeves.

Record Storage Ideas

There are a variety of record-specific storage options that allow you to both store and display your records. No matter what type of record storage you choose, be sure to consider the following:

- How many records can it hold and will that be enough?
- What size is it and will it fit where I want it to go?
- Will records properly sit vertically within the selected storage option?
- Does it offer any protection from the sun?
- Do I need any portable record storage for traveling with my albums?
- What storage solution will fit with my style?

Keeping these questions in mind will ensure you select the right record storage for you. While you can be inventive and find endless original record storage possibilities, these are the most commonly preferred record storage options.

RECORD CARRYING CASE

A record carrying case is a box that includes a handle and closure, perfectly sized for storing records. They are usually sized for 12-, 10-, and 7-inch records. Although this type of storage is best suited for a collection of a few records or for transporting records, it is one of the best ways to store records because it is a closed case, protecting your collection from UV rays, dust, and any other contaminants in your environment. Record carrying cases have existed for years, and uniquely retro cases can be found used on eBay or in antique shops for a fairly reasonable price.

MILK CRATES

Vintage milk crates are a classic way to store vinyl records. In fact, this method was so popular that milk companies modified their

The Milk Crate Crime

In some states, it is illegal to sell or be in possession of a milk crate bearing a company name that is not yours. The intention of milk crates is to allow the dairy industry to transport and deliver milk in an environmentally friendly way. Due to the high number of thefts, various states have imposed laws deeming not only the theft of milk crates illegal, but improperly using them, damaging them, or being in illegal possession of a milk crate can land you in serious trouble.

crate size to try to deter people from stealing their crates for record storage. This has made it quite difficult to find used milk crates that are wide enough for storing records. The good news is that there are crates currently being manufactured that can be purchased legally! The storage company Sterilite currently has two styles of crates that fit both LPs and 7-inch records. These are commonly found at both Walmart and Target stores during the summer months alongside their college storage displays.

OTHER STORAGE CRATES

Although milk crates are the staple record storage crate, there are various other types of boxes and crates available at a reasonable price point. Over the last few years, wooden vintage fruit and wine crates have become quite popular and are readily available at garage sales, flea markets, and antique shops. If you want to try other types of crates, just be sure they adequately fit the records and support them in standing in an upright position, and be sure the wood is in solid condition with no nails or wood chunks sticking out.

WAX STACKS

These are interlocking, collapsible, and customizable record storage bins, similar to crates. No tools are required—you can build these crates in less than a minute by clicking together interlocking pieces. Wax Stacks crates hold about fifty records and are a bit on the pricier side. However, they are worth the money if you can afford them. The crates are stackable, will protect your records while transporting them, and are made from high-quality and sustainable Baltic birch logs.

Record Storage Furniture

A variety of record storage furniture is available, ranging from large entertainment units to side tables with slots for storing records.

VINTAGE OPTIONS

Since vinyl was the primary medium prior to the 1980s, you can often purchase used furniture designed to hold records for reasonable prices at antique shops, thrift stores, garage sales, and on local online marketplaces.

IKEA

Newly designed and manufactured record storage furniture does exist as well. Ikea is the most reliable source for record storage furniture. For countless years, the Ikea Expedit, a cubby-type bookcase shelving system that perfectly fits records, had been a staple piece of record furniture among record collectors. Boasting the ability to hold around 90–100 records per cubby and available in up to twenty-cubby units, the Expedit was a cost-efficient way to store and display your extensive record collection. The Expedit contained either four, eight, sixteen, or twenty cubbies. You could pair them up, store vertically or horizontally, or in extreme cases, stack them twenty cubbies high (while modified to be bolted to a wall, of course).

In 2014, Ikea discontinued the Expedit. Vinyl collectors went crazy, and an Internet fury was launched! Immediately, Expedits were sold out all across North America and other countries. Alongside the announcement, Ikea introduced the Kallax, their updated cubby shelf system with slimmer, sleek edges, as opposed to the sharp edges of the Expedit. Critics of the revised Kallax shelf swore the updated models would be of cheaper quality; however, Ikea notes it has the same properties as the Expedit and can handle the same weight, about 28 pounds per shelf.

Record Frames

Records can be stored and displayed within a record frame. Many types of record frames are available on the market. When purchasing a frame, be sure that it will not damage the record in any way, unless your goal is solely to display the record and not play it. When using a record frame for an extended period, consider that you are potentially exposing the cover of the record to direct UV light while the rest of the album is covered. The cover may discolor if you leave the album in the display frame for quite a while.

Preservation display frames, which contain museum-quality glass, are available. Before purchasing a preservation display frame, verify that the museum glass is UV blocking; this will guarantee your cover is protected from any potential UV damage.

Insuring Your Record Collection

As you build your collection, you may reach a point where you have accumulated a valuable stash of records. At that point, you want to be sure to insure them. There is nothing more horrifying than coming home to find all the contents of your home stolen, or experiencing a horrific tragedy such as a fire or flood and losing personal property—so consider giving yourself some peace of mind when it comes to your vinyl collection.

Perhaps the most common record damaging culprit is water damage from a flood. If you live in an area where storms such as hurricanes or tornadoes occur, do not forget to include your records in your insurance policy. Luckily,

The World's Largest Record Collection

Zero Freitas of Brazil is recognized as the owner of the world's largest record collection, at more than eight million records. Many long-term collectors may recognize him by his anonymous advertisements in *Billboard* magazine that read "RECORD COLLECTIONS. We BUY any record collection. Any style of music. We pay HIGHER prices than anyone else."

insuring a record collection can be accomplished the same way you would insure any of the contents in your home.

UNDERSTAND YOUR INSURANCE POLICY

You may already have a home insurance policy, but it may not include any or all of the total value of your record collection. The first course of action would be to contact your provider and determine if your records are covered. When speaking to your provider, it is best to let your provider know the approximate value of your records so that you can decide on how to best cover the value of your items. Additionally, this conversation with your provider would be an excellent time to review the loss scenarios your coverage would include, such as theft, flood, fire, and so on.

HOW TO DOCUMENT YOUR COLLECTION FOR AN INSURANCE POLICY

While the bulk of your possessions may be reasonably straightforward to replace with insurance funds, you may not be able to find rare records right away, if at all. Plus, if you manage to find them, they may cost much more than you initially purchased them for. To get an accurate calculation of how much it would cost to replace your collection, perform an "appraisal" and provide this to your insurance company. Providing documentation of precisely what you possess and the appraised value will furnish the best possibility of insuring your records for the appropriate amount. Here is how to document your record collection:

- **Keep a log of your collection.** This journal can provide you with a quick and reliable reference of each album you possess, providing a fast and reliable reference if something was ever to happen. The information you log will allow you to easily provide your insurance company with a list of losses and enable you to reference the exact version of an album you have, in turn making it easier to research an accurate value of each record.
- **Value your collection.** Once you have a log of your albums, you can research and provide value to each album.

Discogs.com will provide you with a minimum, median, and maximum price range listed beside each album. If you are looking to insure your albums, the total value can help you gauge if it would be worth insuring your collection or not. If an accident occurs, Discogs can provide you with the current value of each record at that specific time, as well as sources to replace them, if you choose to do that.

- **Verify the most valuable albums.** With your extra-valuable records, check various sources for an assessment on the value of those records, just to be confident you are insured for enough to replace the records. The insurance company will appreciate it if you have multiple sources to validate the amount you are assigning each record. Other reputable sources besides Discogs to verify the value include:
    - **Popsike.com:** Allows you to search certain records and access data on how much they have been sold for on eBay, the primary online auction house for records.
    - **Price guides:** Various published books offer record-pricing guides; these can be purchased at any bookstore or online bookseller.
- **Decide on insurance coverage.** Now that you know the worth of your collection, discussing it with your insurance provider will allow you to best decide how to move forward with insuring your records. In cases where your collection is highly valuable, your provider may request a log of your records and their value. On the anniversary of your policy, be sure to update your records and supply your insurance provider with the updated value of your collection if it significantly changes.

CHAPTER 5

Cleaning and Repairing Records

Both new and used records need cleaning in order to achieve the best sound possible. No matter what sort of contaminant is on your record and why, it can cause pops, clicks, and an unpleasant listening experience. Properly cleaning your records will not only increase their longevity, but will also help to avoid or troubleshoot playback issues. On occasion, you might run into clicks and pops while playing a newly manufactured record—something you can quickly fix by cleaning the record. Not to mention, developing proficient cleaning skills will allow you to pick up used records that can be gems if cleaning is all they require.

Why Do Records Need to Be Cleaned?

Whether your records are new or used, they should always be cleaned before being played on a turntable. You'd want to clean a used record for obvious reasons, such as dirt, dust, and any other contaminants it may have on its surface. New records also require cleaning because they too are often exposed to dirt and dust and can frequently retain a residue from the manufacturing process that is not always visible.

INITIAL CLEANING AND MAINTENANCE

Very dirty records can be challenging to clean. However, once you clean the record, if you control its cleanliness through the following maintenance methods, it is relatively effortless to manage to keep it clean. When you buy a record, it is best to perform an extensive wet cleaning. Following a thorough wet cleaning, you can use a dry-brush method for maintenance, typically completed before and after playing a record.

COMMON CLEANING METHODS

There are two basic methods for cleaning records:

1. Wet cleaning, typically involving a fluid and a brush or record cleaning machine
2. Dry cleaning using a dry brush

Numerous fluids, brushes, and machines are available within all price ranges. A variety of reputable brands, along with instructions for the different methods for cleaning vinyl records, are described in the following sections.

Beware Internet Remedies!

Searching online for record cleaning methods will yield results advising you to clean your records with homemade solutions varying from just water to dish soap, alcohol, and other chemicals commonly found in your home. Avoid all of these methods if your goal is to properly preserve your records for a long time.

Wet Cleaning

You should clean all records, whether new or used, prior to playing using a wet-cleaning method. Wet cleaning a record is done using either a vacuum cleaning machine or a combination of a cleaning solution and a record cleaning brush. Remember, when choosing a brush and fluid, confirm that they are appropriate for the types of materials you are cleaning. Not all fluids and brushes are ideal for shellac records, and certain brushes are not suitable for vinyl records.

There are various methods for cleaning a record, which can primarily be broken down into:

1. A one-step cleaning process, which uses one cleaner to clean the record
2. A two-step cleaning process
3. A three-step cleaning process

Two- and three-step cleaning processes are best done using a vacuum cleaner and are effective for exceedingly problematic contaminants such as cigarette smoke, mold, and mildew. The methods

Skip the Alcohol for Shellac Records

Do not ever clean shellac records with alcohol products! Alcohol will dissolve the shellac compound, permanently damaging your record. Many commercial record cleaners contain alcohol, so when purchasing a cleaner, use only ones you can verify do not contain alcohol.

and options for cleaning records are endless and a bit overwhelming, but following are the tried-and-true methods and products that are simple and effective.

ONE-STEP METHOD: CLEANING BRUSH AND FLUID

Although each manufacturer will have specific instructions on how to use its product, here are the general steps performed in a one-step cleaning method using a brush and fluid:

1. Place the record on a flat surface. Detail-oriented collectors prefer to place the record on a cork or rubber turntable mat with a towel or other absorbent cloth underneath it. If you do not own a turntable mat, make sure that whatever surface you choose to place the record on will not damage the record.
2. Carefully remove any loose dust with a compressed air can, if available.
3. Apply the fluid to the record or brush, whichever the manufacturer advises.
4. Spread the fluid carefully onto the record with the brush.
5. Brush the record. The direction you should brush the record and the amount of pressure to apply, typically gentle, will be specified by the manufacturer of the fluid you're using.
6. When done brushing, allow the record to completely dry before playing it.

TWO- AND THREE-STEP CLEANING METHODS

When buying used records, you may encounter tough-to-clean records, such as those that smell like cigarette smoke. In these instances, using a two- or three-step cleaning method may help clear up these types of issues. Two- and three-step methods are essentially the same as the one-step method, just done two or three times using a different cleaning solution each time. Each solution will address specific contaminants, ensuring a thorough cleaning.

If you buy records that require using a two- or three-step method, check out the Audio Intelligent website (www.audiointelligent.com/products.htm). The site provides comprehensive details on how to perform two- and three-step methods. Audio Intelligent's two- and three-step methods begin with an enzyme-based formula for the first step. This helps loosen and dissolve a variety of contaminants. The second step utilizes their Super Cleaner Formula solution, which targets contaminants that were not removed by the Enzymatic Formula. Audio Intelligent also sells an ultra-pure water that has been deionized and is lab-grade quality, which is best suited for cleaning records.

Don't Feel Overwhelmed

Practicing all the cleaning and protection methods explained in this chapter will keep you confidently collecting records and preserving your music for many years of enjoyment. Even though this chapter includes some really meticulous details on how to care for your collection, don't feel too overwhelmed. Do your best to keep your records relatively clean and you should be fine.

CLEANING BRUSHES AND RECOMMENDED FLUIDS

A cost-effective way to properly clean a record is to use record cleaning fluid, also called RCF, and an appropriate record cleaning brush that is suitable for wet cleaning. When choosing a record cleaning fluid, select one that is manufactured and developed in a laboratory with lab-grade materials and purified water. If water is not purified, it can contain various minerals and other contaminants that can be harmful to your records. If you purchase fluid that needs to be diluted or requires water for record cleaning at any point, use deionized or distilled water to avoid any potential damage. When cleaning your records with a brush and fluid (as opposed to a vacuum-cleaning method), it is best to purchase fluids that do not require rinsing because rinsing a record without a vacuum-cleaning machine can be risky if you're not experienced. Following are record cleaning brush and fluid combinations I recommend.

AUDIO INTELLIGENT PREMIUM ONE-STEP FORMULA NO. 6 WITH LISTENER SELECT 12" BRUSH

Audio Intelligent fluids (www.audiointelligent.com/products.htm) are enzyme-based and manufactured using only lab-grade water distilled six times at their laboratory. The Premium One-Step Formula No. 6 is a no-rinse method that requires you to simply apply the fluid to the record surface with their Listener Select brush (or other flat-bottom brush, such as the Disc Doctor's brush discussed next), to spread the fluid across the record. Next, you gently apply a slight pressure of the brush to the record surface and continue to clean until the solution has dried (approximately 1–3 minutes). This allows the enzymes to loosen and dissolve any contaminants on the record.

THE DISC DOCTOR'S QUICK WASH RECORD CLEANER WITH THE DISC DOCTOR'S MIRACLE RECORD BRUSH SIZE A

The Disc Doctor's brushes are suitable for all types of records, including vinyl, shellac, lacquer, and Edison Diamond Discs (available at www.discdoc.com). The Disc Doctor's flat-bottom brush is particularly good. When combined with the QuickWash Record Cleaner (a blend of purified water and biodegradable surfactants), it is an affordable, highly effective, and simple way to manually clean your records. The QuickWash fluid, which also requires no rinse, is applied to the record by first dispersing the solution onto your brush and using it to gently spread the fluid to the grooved area. It is a remarkably effective and inexpensive way to clean your records.

LAST FACTORY ALL-PURPOSE RECORD CLEANER

The LAST Factory All-Purpose Record Cleaner (www.thelastfactory.com) includes a 2-ounce bottle of fluid and two microfiber applicators. This product is specifically devised to remove residues and contaminants left over from the manufacturing process in addition to everyday dirt, making it an excellent cleaner for newly manufactured records. LAST Factory products are simple to use. You apply a designated number of drops to the included applicator and sweep it along the record, following the grooves, which collects dust particles and other residues directly onto the applicator. You can also purchase applicators separately as needed.

RECORD CLEANING MACHINES

Purchasing a vacuum record cleaning machine, occasionally referred to as an RCM, is the best way to be confident your records are 100 percent clean. There are several record cleaning systems available on the market. If you are investing in a cleaning machine, choose one with a vacuum. When using a vacuum system, the dirt is suctioned off the record—not pushed into the grooves—providing you with a spotless record.

Vacuum record cleaning machines can be costly, although they will last an extremely long time. If purchasing one is not an option, you may also check your local record store or local electronics dealers because they might own a high-quality record cleaning machine and charge patrons a small fee to clean records on it. Here are a few recommended vacuum-type record cleaners:

PRO-JECT VC-S2

Turntable manufacturer Pro-Ject makes a reasonably priced vacuum record cleaner. The machine is very simple to operate: You place the record you wish to clean onto the platter, turn on the machine to start the platter spinning, and while the record spins you add the fluid. You then spread the fluid evenly across the record with a Pro-Ject goat hair brush. You lower the vacuum arm to the record and turn on the vacuum. If you intend to purchase lots of used records, this is an exceptional record cleaning machine at the lowest end of the price range.

NITTY GRITTY

Nitty Gritty has been producing high-quality vacuum record-cleaning machines since the 1980s. Their entry-level machine, the Model 1.0, features manual operations. You apply the fluid to the record on the machine with a brush and manually rotate the platter while the machine vacuums.

As you move up in price to the Nitty Gritty 1.5 and 2.5, the record is automatically rotated during the vacuum cycle. The Fi Models are entirely automatic; however, the record needs to be manually turned over to complete cleaning of both sides.

Nitty Gritty also offers two other models. The 2.5Fi-XP is best utilized for the two-step cleaning method because it can dispense two different fluids interchangeably. The top-of-the-line Nitty Gritty is called the Mini-Pro, and it's fully automatic and cleans both sides of the record at one time. The Mini-Pro 1 is housed in a black woodgrain cabinet, and the Mini-Pro 2 features a cherry finish, solid oak cabinet.

CLEARAUDIO

Clearaudio offers two record cleaning machines for the high-end audiophile who wants to ensure the utmost sound quality and preservation of their records. The Smart Matrix Professional, which cleans each record side individually, requires manual application of the fluid to the record. The Double Matrix Professional Sonic provides 100 percent automatic application or the ability to control any element of the cleaning process using a control panel. In addition to how efficiently it cleans the records, benefits include the ability to adjust the platter spinning direction while cleaning, which ensures clean grooves, and it is significantly less noisy compared to competing record cleaning machines.

VPI

VPI produces two record cleaning devices—the HW-16.5, a manual machine, and the MW-1 Cyclone. The HW-16.5 has been in production for more than thirty years and is a reliable, award-winning system. The MW-1 provides you the ability to clean the record both clockwise and counterclockwise, ensuring a thorough cleaning of the record groove not available on other machines.

SPIN-CLEAN RECORD WASHER MKII

The Spin-Clean is a straightforward machine to operate that acts sort of as a bath for your records. You fill the bottom of the machine with a record cleaning solution and distilled or deionized water, and spin your record through the bath. If you buy a large collection of really dirty old records, the Spin-Clean is a cost-effective way to perform an initial wet cleaning. However, after you run the records through the Spin-Clean, you should perform a second wet cleaning using a brush and fluid combination to make sure the records are thoroughly cleaned.

Antistatic Record Guns

Once you remove the static from the record, the record will collect less dust and other particles. In addition to records, an antistatic gun can be used on film, glass, CDs, DVDs, and lenses. It removes static charges from your records, which may provide a cleaner sound too. You point it at the record from approximately 2–6 inches away, pull the trigger, and slowly release it. One reliable brand is the Zerostat 3 from Milty; it's estimated to last for around 10,000 trigger pulls.

Dry Cleaning

Dry brushes are utilized to maintain record cleanliness. You should use a dry brush before and after playing a record that has been cleaned recently, either with a cleaning machine or the brush and fluid method previously mentioned.

The type of brush you use depends on the kind of record you are playing. When cleaning a polyvinyl "vinyl" record, use a carbon fiber brush. Carbon fiber is strong enough to clear away dirt and soft enough not to cause scratches within the grooves. Using a carbon fiber brush also aids in the removal of static, making it an ideal cleaning tool to use before playing the record. There are countless companies out there that are making dry brushes. Here are the dry brushes that I recommend:

- Pro-Ject Audio Systems Brush It, Antistatic Carbon Fiber Record Brush

- AudioQuest Antistatic Record Brush
- Hunt EDA Mark 6 Carbon Fiber Record Brush

CLEANING SHELLAC, ACETATES, OR EDISON DIAMOND DISCS

To clean shellac, acetates, or Edison Diamond Discs with a dry brush, you need to purchase a brush that is specifically recommended for cleaning these materials, such as the Disc Doctor's Miracle Record Brush Size D.

Record Cleaning Methods to Avoid

Unfortunately, you can find a lot of horrible options for cleaning a record via a simple Internet search. If you are investing effort into cleaning a record, use the brushes and the fluids recommended in this chapter and avoid the risk of damaging your records and turntable. In particular, be sure to stay away from the following methods.

WOOD GLUE

Several years ago, coinciding with the media reports regarding the vinyl boom, a video on YouTube shared a method of cleaning your records using wood glue. In no time, the video went viral, boasting over 1.6 million views! Essentially, the technique involves applying glue to the grooved area of a spinning record. The glue-covered record is set aside to dry overnight. When dry, the glue is manually peeled off, producing a smooth and clean record.

It seems like a good idea, but do not use this method. It is time-consuming, and if you are not patient when removing the glue, you can damage the record. Not to mention, the video advises you to apply glue to a record while it is on your turntable and to smooth it out without getting any on the center label, two actions that are very risky.

DISH SOAP

Cleaning vinyl records with dish soap is a common practice. If you elect to experiment with this method, bear in mind that commercial products and soap compositions have been modified over the years and vary from brand to brand. If you can't determine precisely what chemicals are in your soap and how the vinyl will react to them, it is best to avoid using soap on your records. Another reason to avoid this method is that it is commonly used with tap water and a cloth that may scratch your record. If you possess a reasonably cheap record you are not too concerned with damaging and you experiment with this method, be sure to mix the soap with distilled water and use a record brush or cloth that will not scratch the record.

RECORD CLEANING FLUIDS WITHOUT CLEAR INGREDIENT LISTS

When it comes to buying record cleaning solutions, avoid the ones that provide you little to no information on the ingredients used. If they do not provide you with information on what's in their solution, it is unlikely beneficial for your records, and in certain instances, it can be detrimental. If you come across a cleaning fluid not mentioned in this book, do a bit of research and find reviews written by reputable record collectors before committing to it or using it on valuable records.

How to Fix a Warped Record

Despite your best efforts to maintain your records, sometimes one will warp. Or, you'll buy one that's warped because it's a great find. There are two things you need to flatten a warped record: heat and heavy objects to sandwich the record between. Many websites advise using a stove at a very low temperature, but that can be risky. If possible, wait until the weather is very warm in your area. Then sandwich each album between two heavy books and put the stack into a room that hits warm temperatures (approximately 85°F–90°F). Leave them there for at least a week, longer if possible. Most of the time, this process ensures that the records become unwarped—or at least much less warped and in more of a playable condition.

Fixing Scratches on Records

Although there are many resources claiming that you can fix scratches on a record with sandpaper, ice, and so on, it's often very tricky to make those ideas work. You can find much easier success reducing the noise from scratches and needle drops by using a wet melamine foam brush (Magic Eraser). (Don't try this on a record you are too concerned with losing if this does not work for you.) To test, follow these steps:

1. Thoroughly clean the record using a proper cleaning method such as a two- or three-step method first (see instructions earlier in this chapter).
2. Use deionized or distilled water to wet the melamine foam brush. Squeeze out excess water.
3. Lightly scrub the scratch or needle drop damage with the brush.

This method doesn't always work and is by no means a miracle cure, but it is an option you can try after using all proper cleaning methods.

The other thing to keep in mind about noises caused by scratches is that on occasion, after playing the album a few times, the noise from the scratch can reduce itself on its own and be less noticeable. Regardless, if you are going to purchase many used records, the occasional blemish that causes a second or two of imperfection on an album shouldn't matter that much.

PART 3

MY VINYL JOURNAL

MUST-BUY LIST

STARTS ON PAGE 71

As you learned throughout Part 1, records are not always available to purchase immediately, and you might have to spend some time hunting for special ones you want. Every record collector has a "want" list, and this section will allow you to keep track of yours. Simply jot down titles you'd like to own, and cross them off when you finally acquire them.

When filling out your Must-Buy List, be sure to list the artist's name, the album name, and some pressing details on the version you want. The pressing details can help you identify a specific pressing and can consist of vinyl wax color, release year, unique jacket markings, matrix number, UPC, or anything specific to that release that can quickly help you pinpoint it.

For a refresher on all the ways to recognize a pressing, you can revisit the Identifying the Pressing Version section in Chapter 3.

The White Whale

There is often a "white whale" within a collector's Must-Buy List—a wanted album that is super rare, hard to find, and frequently pricey. Don't worry; many collectors eventually find their white whale, which means you can appoint another desired title as your new white whale.

INDEX OF RECORDS

STARTS ON PAGE 82

This index will allow you to record and track the page number for each album you enter into your Record Log. The order in which you choose to list your records is totally up to you! You can choose to create an index that lists your albums in order of date of purchase, with you updating it as you collect. Or you may decide to wait until the entire Record Log section is complete and list your albums alphabetically.

RECORD LOG

STARTS ON PAGE 120

As you build your collection, this section will allow you to list each record you have and jot down important facts and notes about each one. Here is how you fill out each part of the Record Log:

- **Album Identifiers:** The first part of the log allows you to record the specifics about each of your records—the artist, album title, the year it was released, the country of release, record label, catalog number, and pressing version. This log will help you keep track of your collection, and you can also use this information to keep track of the value of your records as well. If you need assistance locating any of this information on your album, you can review the Identifying the Pressing Version section in Chapter 3.
- **Listening Notes:** The resurgence of vinyl has brought back the art of deeply listening to a full album of music. Completely unplug and listen to your albums, with no distractions, from beginning to end, just as you would watch a movie. Take your time and enjoy the artists' hard work in each note and lyric. When you feel ready, use this section to log any thoughts, feelings, memories, emotions, comments, experiences, or whatever comes to mind.
- **Grading:** Here's where you note the condition of an album. You can use the grade provided to you by the seller, or you can complete your own assessment of the album (using the grading system outlined in Chapter 3) and assign it a grade yourself.

ARTIST	ALBUM TITLE	PRESSING DETAILS

MUST-BUY LIST

ARTIST	ALBUM TITLE	PRESSING DETAILS

ARTIST	ALBUM TITLE	PRESSING DETAILS

MUST-BUY LIST

ARTIST	ALBUM TITLE	PRESSING DETAILS

ARTIST	ALBUM TITLE	PRESSING DETAILS

MUST-BUY LIST

ARTIST	ALBUM TITLE	PRESSING DETAILS

ARTIST	ALBUM TITLE	PRESSING DETAILS

MUST-BUY LIST

ARTIST	ALBUM TITLE	PRESSING DETAILS

ARTIST	ALBUM TITLE	PRESSING DETAILS

MUST-BUY LIST

ARTIST	ALBUM TITLE	PRESSING DETAILS

ARTIST	ALBUM TITLE	PRESSING DETAILS

INDEX OF RECORDS

PAGE #	ARTIST	ALBUM TITLE
120		
120		
120		
121		
121		
121		
122		
122		
122		
123		
123		
123		

PAGE #	ARTIST	ALBUM TITLE
124		
124		
124		
125		
125		
125		
126		
126		
126		
127		
127		
127		

INDEX OF RECORDS

PAGE #	ARTIST	ALBUM TITLE
128		
128		
128		
129		
129		
129		
130		
130		
130		
131		
131		
131		

PAGE #	ARTIST	ALBUM TITLE
132		
132		
132		
133		
133		
133		
134		
134		
134		
135		
135		
135		

INDEX OF RECORDS

PAGE #	ARTIST	ALBUM TITLE
136		
136		
136		
137		
137		
137		
138		
138		
138		
139		
139		
139		

PAGE #	ARTIST	ALBUM TITLE
140		
140		
140		
141		
141		
141		
142		
142		
142		
143		
143		
143		

INDEX OF RECORDS

PAGE #	ARTIST	ALBUM TITLE
144		
144		
144		
145		
145		
145		
146		
146		
146		
147		
147		
147		

PAGE #	ARTIST	ALBUM TITLE
148		
148		
148		
149		
149		
149		
150		
150		
150		
151		
151		
151		

INDEX OF RECORDS

PAGE #	ARTIST	ALBUM TITLE
152		
152		
152		
153		
153		
153		
154		
154		
154		
155		
155		
155		

PAGE #	ARTIST	ALBUM TITLE
156		
156		
156		
157		
157		
157		
158		
158		
158		
159		
159		
159		

INDEX OF RECORDS

PAGE #	ARTIST	ALBUM TITLE
160		
160		
160		
161		
161		
161		
162		
162		
162		
163		
163		
163		

PAGE #	ARTIST	ALBUM TITLE
164		
164		
164		
165		
165		
165		
166		
166		
166		
167		
167		
167		

INDEX OF RECORDS

PAGE #	ARTIST	ALBUM TITLE
168		
168		
168		
169		
169		
169		
170		
170		
170		
171		
171		
171		

PAGE #	ARTIST	ALBUM TITLE
172		
172		
172		
173		
173		
173		
174		
174		
174		
175		
175		
175		

INDEX OF RECORDS

PAGE #	ARTIST	ALBUM TITLE
176		
176		
176		
177		
177		
177		
178		
178		
178		
179		
179		
179		

PAGE #	ARTIST	ALBUM TITLE
180		
180		
180		
181		
181		
181		
182		
182		
182		
183		
183		
183		

INDEX OF RECORDS

PAGE #	ARTIST	ALBUM TITLE
184		
184		
184		
185		
185		
185		
186		
186		
186		
187		
187		
187		

PAGE #	ARTIST	ALBUM TITLE
188		
188		
188		
189		
189		
189		
190		
190		
190		
191		
191		
191		

INDEX OF RECORDS

PAGE #	ARTIST	ALBUM TITLE
192		
192		
192		
193		
193		
193		
194		
194		
194		
195		
195		
195		

PAGE #	ARTIST	ALBUM TITLE
196		
196		
196		
197		
197		
197		
198		
198		
198		
199		
199		
199		

INDEX OF RECORDS

PAGE #	ARTIST	ALBUM TITLE
200		
200		
200		
201		
201		
201		
202		
202		
202		
203		
203		
203		

PAGE #	ARTIST	ALBUM TITLE
204		
204		
204		
205		
205		
205		
206		
206		
206		
207		
207		
207		

INDEX OF RECORDS

PAGE #	ARTIST	ALBUM TITLE
208		
208		
208		
209		
209		
209		
210		
210		
210		
211		
211		
211		

PAGE #	ARTIST	ALBUM TITLE
212		
212		
212		
213		
213		
213		
214		
214		
214		
215		
215		
215		

INDEX OF RECORDS

PAGE #	ARTIST	ALBUM TITLE
216		
216		
216		
217		
217		
217		
218		
218		
218		
219		
219		
219		

PAGE #	ARTIST	ALBUM TITLE
220		
220		
220		
221		
221		
221		
222		
222		
222		
223		
223		
223		

INDEX OF RECORDS

PAGE #	ARTIST	ALBUM TITLE
224		
224		
224		
225		
225		
225		
226		
226		
226		
227		
227		
227		

PAGE #	ARTIST	ALBUM TITLE
228		
228		
228		
229		
229		
229		
230		
230		
230		
231		
231		
231		

INDEX OF RECORDS

PAGE #	ARTIST	ALBUM TITLE
232		
232		
232		
233		
233		
233		
234		
234		
234		
235		
235		
235		

PAGE #	ARTIST	ALBUM TITLE
236		
236		
236		
237		
237		
237		
238		
238		
238		
239		
239		
239		

INDEX OF RECORDS

PAGE #	ARTIST	ALBUM TITLE
240		
240		
240		
241		
241		
241		
242		
242		
242		
243		
243		
243		

PAGE #	ARTIST	ALBUM TITLE
244		
244		
244		
245		
245		
245		
246		
246		
246		
247		
247		
247		

INDEX OF RECORDS

PAGE #	ARTIST	ALBUM TITLE
248		
248		
248		
249		
249		
249		
250		
250		
250		
251		
251		
251		

PAGE #	ARTIST	ALBUM TITLE
252		
252		
252		
253		
253		
253		
254		
254		
254		
255		
255		
255		

INDEX OF RECORDS

PAGE #	ARTIST	ALBUM TITLE
256		
256		
256		
257		
257		
257		
258		
258		
258		
259		
259		
259		

PAGE #	ARTIST	ALBUM TITLE
260		
260		
260		
261		
261		
261		
262		
262		
262		
263		
263		
263		

INDEX OF RECORDS

PAGE #	ARTIST	ALBUM TITLE
264		
264		
264		
265		
265		
265		
266		
266		
266		
267		
267		
267		

PAGE #	ARTIST	ALBUM TITLE
268		
268		
268		
269		
269		
269		
270		
270		
270		
271		
271		
271		

RECORD LOG

ARTIST	ALBUM
YEAR / COUNTRY	LABEL
CATALOG NUMBER	PRESSING VERSION

LISTENING NOTES

GRADING: SS M NM VG+ VG G+ G F P

ARTIST	ALBUM
YEAR / COUNTRY	LABEL
CATALOG NUMBER	PRESSING VERSION

LISTENING NOTES

GRADING: SS M NM VG+ VG G+ G F P

ARTIST	ALBUM
YEAR / COUNTRY	LABEL
CATALOG NUMBER	PRESSING VERSION

LISTENING NOTES

GRADING: SS M NM VG+ VG G+ G F P

ARTIST	ALBUM
YEAR / COUNTRY	LABEL
CATALOG NUMBER	PRESSING VERSION

LISTENING NOTES

GRADING: SS M NM VG+ VG G+ G F P

ARTIST	ALBUM
YEAR / COUNTRY	LABEL
CATALOG NUMBER	PRESSING VERSION

LISTENING NOTES

GRADING: SS M NM VG+ VG G+ G F P

ARTIST	ALBUM
YEAR / COUNTRY	LABEL
CATALOG NUMBER	PRESSING VERSION

LISTENING NOTES

GRADING: SS M NM VG+ VG G+ G F P

RECORD LOG

ARTIST	ALBUM
YEAR / COUNTRY	LABEL
CATALOG NUMBER	PRESSING VERSION

LISTENING NOTES

GRADING: SS M NM VG+ VG G+ G F P

ARTIST	ALBUM
YEAR / COUNTRY	LABEL
CATALOG NUMBER	PRESSING VERSION

LISTENING NOTES

GRADING: SS M NM VG+ VG G+ G F P

ARTIST	ALBUM
YEAR / COUNTRY	LABEL
CATALOG NUMBER	PRESSING VERSION

LISTENING NOTES

GRADING: SS M NM VG+ VG G+ G F P

ARTIST	ALBUM
YEAR / COUNTRY	LABEL
CATALOG NUMBER	PRESSING VERSION

LISTENING NOTES

GRADING: SS M NM VG+ VG G+ G F P

ARTIST	ALBUM
YEAR / COUNTRY	LABEL
CATALOG NUMBER	PRESSING VERSION

LISTENING NOTES

GRADING: SS M NM VG+ VG G+ G F P

ARTIST	ALBUM
YEAR / COUNTRY	LABEL
CATALOG NUMBER	PRESSING VERSION

LISTENING NOTES

GRADING: SS M NM VG+ VG G+ G F P

RECORD LOG

ARTIST	ALBUM
YEAR / COUNTRY	LABEL
CATALOG NUMBER	PRESSING VERSION

LISTENING NOTES

GRADING: SS M NM VG+ VG G+ G F P

ARTIST	ALBUM
YEAR / COUNTRY	LABEL
CATALOG NUMBER	PRESSING VERSION

LISTENING NOTES

GRADING: SS M NM VG+ VG G+ G F P

ARTIST	ALBUM
YEAR / COUNTRY	LABEL
CATALOG NUMBER	PRESSING VERSION

LISTENING NOTES

GRADING: SS M NM VG+ VG G+ G F P

ARTIST	ALBUM
YEAR / COUNTRY	LABEL
CATALOG NUMBER	PRESSING VERSION

LISTENING NOTES

GRADING: SS M NM VG+ VG G+ G F P

ARTIST	ALBUM
YEAR / COUNTRY	LABEL
CATALOG NUMBER	PRESSING VERSION

LISTENING NOTES

GRADING: SS M NM VG+ VG G+ G F P

ARTIST	ALBUM
YEAR / COUNTRY	LABEL
CATALOG NUMBER	PRESSING VERSION

LISTENING NOTES

GRADING: SS M NM VG+ VG G+ G F P

RECORD LOG

ARTIST	ALBUM
YEAR / COUNTRY	LABEL
CATALOG NUMBER	PRESSING VERSION

LISTENING NOTES

GRADING: SS M NM VG+ VG G+ G F P

ARTIST	ALBUM
YEAR / COUNTRY	LABEL
CATALOG NUMBER	PRESSING VERSION

LISTENING NOTES

GRADING: SS M NM VG+ VG G+ G F P

ARTIST	ALBUM
YEAR / COUNTRY	LABEL
CATALOG NUMBER	PRESSING VERSION

LISTENING NOTES

GRADING: SS M NM VG+ VG G+ G F P

ARTIST	ALBUM
YEAR / COUNTRY	LABEL
CATALOG NUMBER	PRESSING VERSION

LISTENING NOTES

GRADING: SS M NM VG+ VG G+ G F P

ARTIST	ALBUM
YEAR / COUNTRY	LABEL
CATALOG NUMBER	PRESSING VERSION

LISTENING NOTES

GRADING: SS M NM VG+ VG G+ G F P

ARTIST	ALBUM
YEAR / COUNTRY	LABEL
CATALOG NUMBER	PRESSING VERSION

LISTENING NOTES

GRADING: SS M NM VG+ VG G+ G F P

RECORD LOG

ARTIST	ALBUM
YEAR / COUNTRY	LABEL
CATALOG NUMBER	PRESSING VERSION

LISTENING NOTES

GRADING: SS M NM VG+ VG G+ G F P

ARTIST	ALBUM
YEAR / COUNTRY	LABEL
CATALOG NUMBER	PRESSING VERSION

LISTENING NOTES

GRADING: SS M NM VG+ VG G+ G F P

ARTIST	ALBUM
YEAR / COUNTRY	LABEL
CATALOG NUMBER	PRESSING VERSION

LISTENING NOTES

GRADING: SS M NM VG+ VG G+ G F P

ARTIST	ALBUM
YEAR / COUNTRY	LABEL
CATALOG NUMBER	PRESSING VERSION

LISTENING NOTES

GRADING: SS M NM VG+ VG G+ G F P

ARTIST	ALBUM
YEAR / COUNTRY	LABEL
CATALOG NUMBER	PRESSING VERSION

LISTENING NOTES

GRADING: SS M NM VG+ VG G+ G F P

ARTIST	ALBUM
YEAR / COUNTRY	LABEL
CATALOG NUMBER	PRESSING VERSION

LISTENING NOTES

GRADING: SS M NM VG+ VG G+ G F P

RECORD LOG

ARTIST	ALBUM
YEAR / COUNTRY	LABEL
CATALOG NUMBER	PRESSING VERSION

LISTENING NOTES

GRADING: SS M NM VG+ VG G+ G F P

ARTIST	ALBUM
YEAR / COUNTRY	LABEL
CATALOG NUMBER	PRESSING VERSION

LISTENING NOTES

GRADING: SS M NM VG+ VG G+ G F P

ARTIST	ALBUM
YEAR / COUNTRY	LABEL
CATALOG NUMBER	PRESSING VERSION

LISTENING NOTES

GRADING: SS M NM VG+ VG G+ G F P

ARTIST	ALBUM
YEAR / COUNTRY	LABEL
CATALOG NUMBER	PRESSING VERSION

LISTENING NOTES

GRADING: SS M NM VG+ VG G+ G F P

ARTIST	ALBUM
YEAR / COUNTRY	LABEL
CATALOG NUMBER	PRESSING VERSION

LISTENING NOTES

GRADING: SS M NM VG+ VG G+ G F P

ARTIST	ALBUM
YEAR / COUNTRY	LABEL
CATALOG NUMBER	PRESSING VERSION

LISTENING NOTES

GRADING: SS M NM VG+ VG G+ G F P

RECORD LOG

ARTIST	ALBUM
YEAR / COUNTRY	LABEL
CATALOG NUMBER	PRESSING VERSION
LISTENING NOTES	

GRADING: SS M NM VG+ VG G+ G F P

ARTIST	ALBUM
YEAR / COUNTRY	LABEL
CATALOG NUMBER	PRESSING VERSION
LISTENING NOTES	

GRADING: SS M NM VG+ VG G+ G F P

ARTIST	ALBUM
YEAR / COUNTRY	LABEL
CATALOG NUMBER	PRESSING VERSION
LISTENING NOTES	

GRADING: SS M NM VG+ VG G+ G F P

ARTIST	ALBUM
YEAR / COUNTRY	LABEL
CATALOG NUMBER	PRESSING VERSION

LISTENING NOTES

GRADING: SS M NM VG+ VG G+ G F P

ARTIST	ALBUM
YEAR / COUNTRY	LABEL
CATALOG NUMBER	PRESSING VERSION

LISTENING NOTES

GRADING: SS M NM VG+ VG G+ G F P

ARTIST	ALBUM
YEAR / COUNTRY	LABEL
CATALOG NUMBER	PRESSING VERSION

LISTENING NOTES

GRADING: SS M NM VG+ VG G+ G F P

RECORD LOG

ARTIST	ALBUM
YEAR / COUNTRY	LABEL
CATALOG NUMBER	PRESSING VERSION

LISTENING NOTES

GRADING: SS M NM VG+ VG G+ G F P

ARTIST	ALBUM
YEAR / COUNTRY	LABEL
CATALOG NUMBER	PRESSING VERSION

LISTENING NOTES

GRADING: SS M NM VG+ VG G+ G F P

ARTIST	ALBUM
YEAR / COUNTRY	LABEL
CATALOG NUMBER	PRESSING VERSION

LISTENING NOTES

GRADING: SS M NM VG+ VG G+ G F P

ARTIST	ALBUM
YEAR / COUNTRY	LABEL
CATALOG NUMBER	PRESSING VERSION

LISTENING NOTES

GRADING: SS M NM VG+ VG G+ G F P

ARTIST	ALBUM
YEAR / COUNTRY	LABEL
CATALOG NUMBER	PRESSING VERSION

LISTENING NOTES

GRADING: SS M NM VG+ VG G+ G F P

ARTIST	ALBUM
YEAR / COUNTRY	LABEL
CATALOG NUMBER	PRESSING VERSION

LISTENING NOTES

GRADING: SS M NM VG+ VG G+ G F P

RECORD LOG

ARTIST	ALBUM
YEAR / COUNTRY	LABEL
CATALOG NUMBER	PRESSING VERSION

LISTENING NOTES

GRADING: SS M NM VG+ VG G+ G F P

ARTIST	ALBUM
YEAR / COUNTRY	LABEL
CATALOG NUMBER	PRESSING VERSION

LISTENING NOTES

GRADING: SS M NM VG+ VG G+ G F P

ARTIST	ALBUM
YEAR / COUNTRY	LABEL
CATALOG NUMBER	PRESSING VERSION

LISTENING NOTES

GRADING: SS M NM VG+ VG G+ G F P

ARTIST	ALBUM
YEAR / COUNTRY	LABEL
CATALOG NUMBER	PRESSING VERSION

LISTENING NOTES

GRADING: SS M NM VG+ VG G+ G F P

ARTIST	ALBUM
YEAR / COUNTRY	LABEL
CATALOG NUMBER	PRESSING VERSION

LISTENING NOTES

GRADING: SS M NM VG+ VG G+ G F P

ARTIST	ALBUM
YEAR / COUNTRY	LABEL
CATALOG NUMBER	PRESSING VERSION

LISTENING NOTES

GRADING: SS M NM VG+ VG G+ G F P

RECORD LOG

ARTIST	ALBUM
YEAR / COUNTRY	LABEL
CATALOG NUMBER	PRESSING VERSION

LISTENING NOTES

GRADING: SS M NM VG+ VG G+ G F P

ARTIST	ALBUM
YEAR / COUNTRY	LABEL
CATALOG NUMBER	PRESSING VERSION

LISTENING NOTES

GRADING: SS M NM VG+ VG G+ G F P

ARTIST	ALBUM
YEAR / COUNTRY	LABEL
CATALOG NUMBER	PRESSING VERSION

LISTENING NOTES

ARTIST	ALBUM
YEAR / COUNTRY	LABEL
CATALOG NUMBER	PRESSING VERSION

LISTENING NOTES

GRADING: SS M NM VG+ VG G+ G F P

ARTIST	ALBUM
YEAR / COUNTRY	LABEL
CATALOG NUMBER	PRESSING VERSION

LISTENING NOTES

GRADING: SS M NM VG+ VG G+ G F P

ARTIST	ALBUM
YEAR / COUNTRY	LABEL
CATALOG NUMBER	PRESSING VERSION

LISTENING NOTES

GRADING: SS M NM VG+ VG G+ G F P

RECORD LOG

ARTIST	ALBUM
YEAR / COUNTRY	LABEL
CATALOG NUMBER	PRESSING VERSION

LISTENING NOTES

GRADING: ○ SS ○ M ○ NM ○ VG+ ○ VG ○ G+ ○ G ○ F ○ P

ARTIST	ALBUM
YEAR / COUNTRY	LABEL
CATALOG NUMBER	PRESSING VERSION

LISTENING NOTES

GRADING: ○ SS ○ M ○ NM ○ VG+ ○ VG ○ G+ ○ G ○ F ○ P

ARTIST	ALBUM
YEAR / COUNTRY	LABEL
CATALOG NUMBER	PRESSING VERSION

LISTENING NOTES

GRADING: ○ SS ○ M ○ NM ○ VG+ ○ VG ○ G+ ○ G ○ F ○ P

ARTIST	ALBUM
YEAR / COUNTRY	LABEL
CATALOG NUMBER	PRESSING VERSION

LISTENING NOTES

GRADING: SS M NM VG+ VG G+ G F P

ARTIST	ALBUM
YEAR / COUNTRY	LABEL
CATALOG NUMBER	PRESSING VERSION

LISTENING NOTES

GRADING: SS M NM VG+ VG G+ G F P

ARTIST	ALBUM
YEAR / COUNTRY	LABEL
CATALOG NUMBER	PRESSING VERSION

LISTENING NOTES

GRADING: SS M NM VG+ VG G+ G F P

RECORD LOG

ARTIST	ALBUM
YEAR / COUNTRY	LABEL
CATALOG NUMBER	PRESSING VERSION

LISTENING NOTES

GRADING: SS M NM VG+ VG G+ G F P

ARTIST	ALBUM
YEAR / COUNTRY	LABEL
CATALOG NUMBER	PRESSING VERSION

LISTENING NOTES

GRADING: SS M NM VG+ VG G+ G F P

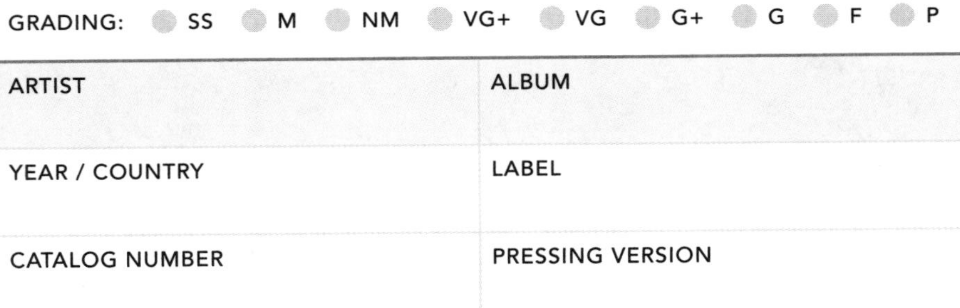

ARTIST	ALBUM
YEAR / COUNTRY	LABEL
CATALOG NUMBER	PRESSING VERSION

LISTENING NOTES

GRADING: SS M NM VG+ VG G+ G F P

ARTIST	ALBUM
YEAR / COUNTRY	LABEL
CATALOG NUMBER	PRESSING VERSION

LISTENING NOTES

GRADING: SS M NM VG+ VG G+ G F P

ARTIST	ALBUM
YEAR / COUNTRY	LABEL
CATALOG NUMBER	PRESSING VERSION

LISTENING NOTES

GRADING: SS M NM VG+ VG G+ G F P

ARTIST	ALBUM
YEAR / COUNTRY	LABEL
CATALOG NUMBER	PRESSING VERSION

LISTENING NOTES

GRADING: SS M NM VG+ VG G+ G F P

RECORD LOG

ARTIST	ALBUM
YEAR / COUNTRY	LABEL
CATALOG NUMBER	PRESSING VERSION

LISTENING NOTES

GRADING: SS M NM VG+ VG G+ G F P

ARTIST	ALBUM
YEAR / COUNTRY	LABEL
CATALOG NUMBER	PRESSING VERSION

LISTENING NOTES

GRADING: SS M NM VG+ VG G+ G F P

ARTIST	ALBUM
YEAR / COUNTRY	LABEL
CATALOG NUMBER	PRESSING VERSION

LISTENING NOTES

GRADING: SS M NM VG+ VG G+ G F P

ARTIST	ALBUM
YEAR / COUNTRY	LABEL
CATALOG NUMBER	PRESSING VERSION

LISTENING NOTES

GRADING: SS M NM VG+ VG G+ G F P

ARTIST	ALBUM
YEAR / COUNTRY	LABEL
CATALOG NUMBER	PRESSING VERSION

LISTENING NOTES

GRADING: SS M NM VG+ VG G+ G F P

ARTIST	ALBUM
YEAR / COUNTRY	LABEL
CATALOG NUMBER	PRESSING VERSION

LISTENING NOTES

GRADING: SS M NM VG+ VG G+ G F P

RECORD LOG

ARTIST	ALBUM
YEAR / COUNTRY	LABEL
CATALOG NUMBER	PRESSING VERSION
LISTENING NOTES	

GRADING: SS M NM VG+ VG G+ G F P

ARTIST	ALBUM
YEAR / COUNTRY	LABEL
CATALOG NUMBER	PRESSING VERSION
LISTENING NOTES	

GRADING: SS M NM VG+ VG G+ G F P

ARTIST	ALBUM
YEAR / COUNTRY	LABEL
CATALOG NUMBER	PRESSING VERSION
LISTENING NOTES	

GRADING: SS M NM VG+ VG G+ G F P

ARTIST	ALBUM
YEAR / COUNTRY	LABEL
CATALOG NUMBER	PRESSING VERSION

LISTENING NOTES

GRADING: SS M NM VG+ VG G+ G F P

ARTIST	ALBUM
YEAR / COUNTRY	LABEL
CATALOG NUMBER	PRESSING VERSION

LISTENING NOTES

GRADING: SS M NM VG+ VG G+ G F P

ARTIST	ALBUM
YEAR / COUNTRY	LABEL
CATALOG NUMBER	PRESSING VERSION

LISTENING NOTES

GRADING: SS M NM VG+ VG G+ G F P

RECORD LOG

ARTIST	ALBUM
YEAR / COUNTRY	LABEL
CATALOG NUMBER	PRESSING VERSION

LISTENING NOTES

GRADING: SS M NM VG+ VG G+ G F P

ARTIST	ALBUM
YEAR / COUNTRY	LABEL
CATALOG NUMBER	PRESSING VERSION

LISTENING NOTES

GRADING: SS M NM VG+ VG G+ G F P

ARTIST	ALBUM
YEAR / COUNTRY	LABEL
CATALOG NUMBER	PRESSING VERSION

LISTENING NOTES

GRADING: SS M NM VG+ VG G+ G F P

ARTIST	ALBUM
YEAR / COUNTRY	LABEL
CATALOG NUMBER	PRESSING VERSION

LISTENING NOTES

GRADING: SS M NM VG+ VG G+ G F P

ARTIST	ALBUM
YEAR / COUNTRY	LABEL
CATALOG NUMBER	PRESSING VERSION

LISTENING NOTES

GRADING: SS M NM VG+ VG G+ G F P

ARTIST	ALBUM
YEAR / COUNTRY	LABEL
CATALOG NUMBER	PRESSING VERSION

LISTENING NOTES

GRADING: SS M NM VG+ VG G+ G F P

RECORD LOG

ARTIST	ALBUM
YEAR / COUNTRY	LABEL
CATALOG NUMBER	PRESSING VERSION

LISTENING NOTES

GRADING: SS M NM VG+ VG G+ G F P

ARTIST	ALBUM
YEAR / COUNTRY	LABEL
CATALOG NUMBER	PRESSING VERSION

LISTENING NOTES

GRADING: SS M NM VG+ VG G+ G F P

ARTIST	ALBUM
YEAR / COUNTRY	LABEL
CATALOG NUMBER	PRESSING VERSION

LISTENING NOTES

GRADING: SS M NM VG+ VG G+ G F P

ARTIST	ALBUM
YEAR / COUNTRY	LABEL
CATALOG NUMBER	PRESSING VERSION

LISTENING NOTES

GRADING: SS M NM VG+ VG G+ G F P

ARTIST	ALBUM
YEAR / COUNTRY	LABEL
CATALOG NUMBER	PRESSING VERSION

LISTENING NOTES

GRADING: SS M NM VG+ VG G+ G F P

ARTIST	ALBUM
YEAR / COUNTRY	LABEL
CATALOG NUMBER	PRESSING VERSION

LISTENING NOTES

GRADING: SS M NM VG+ VG G+ G F P

RECORD LOG

ARTIST	ALBUM
YEAR / COUNTRY	LABEL
CATALOG NUMBER	PRESSING VERSION

LISTENING NOTES

GRADING: SS M NM VG+ VG G+ G F P

ARTIST	ALBUM
YEAR / COUNTRY	LABEL
CATALOG NUMBER	PRESSING VERSION

LISTENING NOTES

GRADING: SS M NM VG+ VG G+ G F P

ARTIST	ALBUM
YEAR / COUNTRY	LABEL
CATALOG NUMBER	PRESSING VERSION

LISTENING NOTES

GRADING: SS M NM VG+ VG G+ G F P

ARTIST	ALBUM
YEAR / COUNTRY	LABEL
CATALOG NUMBER	PRESSING VERSION

LISTENING NOTES

GRADING: SS M NM VG+ VG G+ G F P

ARTIST	ALBUM
YEAR / COUNTRY	LABEL
CATALOG NUMBER	PRESSING VERSION

LISTENING NOTES

GRADING: SS M NM VG+ VG G+ G F P

ARTIST	ALBUM
YEAR / COUNTRY	LABEL
CATALOG NUMBER	PRESSING VERSION

LISTENING NOTES

GRADING: SS M NM VG+ VG G+ G F P

RECORD LOG

ARTIST	ALBUM
YEAR / COUNTRY	LABEL
CATALOG NUMBER	PRESSING VERSION

LISTENING NOTES

GRADING: SS M NM VG+ VG G+ G F P

ARTIST	ALBUM
YEAR / COUNTRY	LABEL
CATALOG NUMBER	PRESSING VERSION

LISTENING NOTES

GRADING: SS M NM VG+ VG G+ G F P

ARTIST	ALBUM
YEAR / COUNTRY	LABEL
CATALOG NUMBER	PRESSING VERSION

LISTENING NOTES

GRADING: SS M NM VG+ VG G+ G F P

ARTIST	ALBUM
YEAR / COUNTRY	LABEL
CATALOG NUMBER	PRESSING VERSION

LISTENING NOTES

GRADING: SS M NM VG+ VG G+ G F P

ARTIST	ALBUM
YEAR / COUNTRY	LABEL
CATALOG NUMBER	PRESSING VERSION

LISTENING NOTES

GRADING: SS M NM VG+ VG G+ G F P

ARTIST	ALBUM
YEAR / COUNTRY	LABEL
CATALOG NUMBER	PRESSING VERSION

LISTENING NOTES

GRADING: SS M NM VG+ VG G+ G F P

RECORD LOG

ARTIST	ALBUM
YEAR / COUNTRY	LABEL
CATALOG NUMBER	PRESSING VERSION

LISTENING NOTES

GRADING: SS M NM VG+ VG G+ G F P

ARTIST	ALBUM
YEAR / COUNTRY	LABEL
CATALOG NUMBER	PRESSING VERSION

LISTENING NOTES

GRADING: SS M NM VG+ VG G+ G F P

ARTIST	ALBUM
YEAR / COUNTRY	LABEL
CATALOG NUMBER	PRESSING VERSION

LISTENING NOTES

GRADING: SS M NM VG+ VG G+ G F P

ARTIST	ALBUM
YEAR / COUNTRY	LABEL
CATALOG NUMBER	PRESSING VERSION

LISTENING NOTES

GRADING: SS M NM VG+ VG G+ G F P

ARTIST	ALBUM
YEAR / COUNTRY	LABEL
CATALOG NUMBER	PRESSING VERSION

LISTENING NOTES

GRADING: SS M NM VG+ VG G+ G F P

ARTIST	ALBUM
YEAR / COUNTRY	LABEL
CATALOG NUMBER	PRESSING VERSION

LISTENING NOTES

GRADING: SS M NM VG+ VG G+ G F P

RECORD LOG

ARTIST	ALBUM
YEAR / COUNTRY	LABEL
CATALOG NUMBER	PRESSING VERSION

LISTENING NOTES

GRADING: SS M NM VG+ VG G+ G F P

ARTIST	ALBUM
YEAR / COUNTRY	LABEL
CATALOG NUMBER	PRESSING VERSION

LISTENING NOTES

GRADING: SS M NM VG+ VG G+ G F P

ARTIST	ALBUM
YEAR / COUNTRY	LABEL
CATALOG NUMBER	PRESSING VERSION

LISTENING NOTES

GRADING: SS M NM VG+ VG G+ G F P

ARTIST	ALBUM
YEAR / COUNTRY	LABEL
CATALOG NUMBER	PRESSING VERSION

LISTENING NOTES

GRADING: SS M NM VG+ VG G+ G F P

ARTIST	ALBUM
YEAR / COUNTRY	LABEL
CATALOG NUMBER	PRESSING VERSION

LISTENING NOTES

GRADING: SS M NM VG+ VG G+ G F P

ARTIST	ALBUM
YEAR / COUNTRY	LABEL
CATALOG NUMBER	PRESSING VERSION

LISTENING NOTES

GRADING: SS M NM VG+ VG G+ G F P

RECORD LOG

ARTIST	ALBUM
YEAR / COUNTRY	LABEL
CATALOG NUMBER	PRESSING VERSION

LISTENING NOTES

GRADING: SS M NM VG+ VG G+ G F P

ARTIST	ALBUM
YEAR / COUNTRY	LABEL
CATALOG NUMBER	PRESSING VERSION

LISTENING NOTES

GRADING: SS M NM VG+ VG G+ G F P

ARTIST	ALBUM
YEAR / COUNTRY	LABEL
CATALOG NUMBER	PRESSING VERSION

LISTENING NOTES

GRADING: SS M NM VG+ VG G+ G F P

ARTIST	ALBUM
YEAR / COUNTRY	LABEL
CATALOG NUMBER	PRESSING VERSION

LISTENING NOTES

GRADING: SS M NM VG+ VG G+ G F P

ARTIST	ALBUM
YEAR / COUNTRY	LABEL
CATALOG NUMBER	PRESSING VERSION

LISTENING NOTES

GRADING: SS M NM VG+ VG G+ G F P

ARTIST	ALBUM
YEAR / COUNTRY	LABEL
CATALOG NUMBER	PRESSING VERSION

LISTENING NOTES

GRADING: SS M NM VG+ VG G+ G F P

RECORD LOG

ARTIST	ALBUM
YEAR / COUNTRY	LABEL
CATALOG NUMBER	PRESSING VERSION

LISTENING NOTES

GRADING: SS M NM VG+ VG G+ G F P

ARTIST	ALBUM
YEAR / COUNTRY	LABEL
CATALOG NUMBER	PRESSING VERSION

LISTENING NOTES

GRADING: SS M NM VG+ VG G+ G F P

ARTIST	ALBUM
YEAR / COUNTRY	LABEL
CATALOG NUMBER	PRESSING VERSION

LISTENING NOTES

GRADING: SS M NM VG+ VG G+ G F P

ARTIST	ALBUM
YEAR / COUNTRY	LABEL
CATALOG NUMBER	PRESSING VERSION

LISTENING NOTES

GRADING: SS M NM VG+ VG G+ G F P

ARTIST	ALBUM
YEAR / COUNTRY	LABEL
CATALOG NUMBER	PRESSING VERSION

LISTENING NOTES

GRADING: SS M NM VG+ VG G+ G F P

ARTIST	ALBUM
YEAR / COUNTRY	LABEL
CATALOG NUMBER	PRESSING VERSION

LISTENING NOTES

GRADING: SS M NM VG+ VG G+ G F P

RECORD LOG

ARTIST	ALBUM
YEAR / COUNTRY	LABEL
CATALOG NUMBER	PRESSING VERSION

LISTENING NOTES

GRADING: SS M NM VG+ VG G+ G F P

ARTIST	ALBUM
YEAR / COUNTRY	LABEL
CATALOG NUMBER	PRESSING VERSION

LISTENING NOTES

GRADING: SS M NM VG+ VG G+ G F P

ARTIST	ALBUM
YEAR / COUNTRY	LABEL
CATALOG NUMBER	PRESSING VERSION

LISTENING NOTES

GRADING: SS M NM VG+ VG G+ G F P

ARTIST	ALBUM
YEAR / COUNTRY	LABEL
CATALOG NUMBER	PRESSING VERSION

LISTENING NOTES

GRADING: SS M NM VG+ VG G+ G F P

ARTIST	ALBUM
YEAR / COUNTRY	LABEL
CATALOG NUMBER	PRESSING VERSION

LISTENING NOTES

GRADING: SS M NM VG+ VG G+ G F P

ARTIST	ALBUM
YEAR / COUNTRY	LABEL
CATALOG NUMBER	PRESSING VERSION

LISTENING NOTES

GRADING: SS M NM VG+ VG G+ G F P

RECORD LOG

ARTIST	ALBUM
YEAR / COUNTRY	LABEL
CATALOG NUMBER	PRESSING VERSION

LISTENING NOTES

GRADING: SS M NM VG+ VG G+ G F P

ARTIST	ALBUM
YEAR / COUNTRY	LABEL
CATALOG NUMBER	PRESSING VERSION

LISTENING NOTES

GRADING: SS M NM VG+ VG G+ G F P

ARTIST	ALBUM
YEAR / COUNTRY	LABEL
CATALOG NUMBER	PRESSING VERSION

LISTENING NOTES

GRADING: SS M NM VG+ VG G+ G F P

ARTIST	ALBUM
YEAR / COUNTRY	LABEL
CATALOG NUMBER	PRESSING VERSION

LISTENING NOTES

GRADING: SS M NM VG+ VG G+ G F P

ARTIST	ALBUM
YEAR / COUNTRY	LABEL
CATALOG NUMBER	PRESSING VERSION

LISTENING NOTES

GRADING: SS M NM VG+ VG G+ G F P

ARTIST	ALBUM
YEAR / COUNTRY	LABEL
CATALOG NUMBER	PRESSING VERSION

LISTENING NOTES

GRADING: SS M NM VG+ VG G+ G F P

RECORD LOG

ARTIST	ALBUM
YEAR / COUNTRY	LABEL
CATALOG NUMBER	PRESSING VERSION

LISTENING NOTES

GRADING: SS M NM VG+ VG G+ G F P

ARTIST	ALBUM
YEAR / COUNTRY	LABEL
CATALOG NUMBER	PRESSING VERSION

LISTENING NOTES

GRADING: SS M NM VG+ VG G+ G F P

ARTIST	ALBUM
YEAR / COUNTRY	LABEL
CATALOG NUMBER	PRESSING VERSION

LISTENING NOTES

GRADING: SS M NM VG+ VG G+ G F P

ARTIST | ALBUM

YEAR / COUNTRY | LABEL

CATALOG NUMBER | PRESSING VERSION

LISTENING NOTES

GRADING: SS M NM VG+ VG G+ G F P

ARTIST | ALBUM

YEAR / COUNTRY | LABEL

CATALOG NUMBER | PRESSING VERSION

LISTENING NOTES

GRADING: SS M NM VG+ VG G+ G F P

ARTIST | ALBUM

YEAR / COUNTRY | LABEL

CATALOG NUMBER | PRESSING VERSION

LISTENING NOTES

GRADING: SS M NM VG+ VG G+ G F P

RECORD LOG

ARTIST	ALBUM
YEAR / COUNTRY	LABEL
CATALOG NUMBER	PRESSING VERSION

LISTENING NOTES

GRADING: SS M NM VG+ VG G+ G F P

ARTIST	ALBUM
YEAR / COUNTRY	LABEL
CATALOG NUMBER	PRESSING VERSION

LISTENING NOTES

GRADING: SS M NM VG+ VG G+ G F P

ARTIST	ALBUM
YEAR / COUNTRY	LABEL
CATALOG NUMBER	PRESSING VERSION

LISTENING NOTES

GRADING: SS M NM VG+ VG G+ G F P

ARTIST	ALBUM
YEAR / COUNTRY	LABEL
CATALOG NUMBER	PRESSING VERSION

LISTENING NOTES

GRADING: SS M NM VG+ VG G+ G F P

ARTIST	ALBUM
YEAR / COUNTRY	LABEL
CATALOG NUMBER	PRESSING VERSION

LISTENING NOTES

GRADING: SS M NM VG+ VG G+ G F P

ARTIST	ALBUM
YEAR / COUNTRY	LABEL
CATALOG NUMBER	PRESSING VERSION

LISTENING NOTES

GRADING: SS M NM VG+ VG G+ G F P

RECORD LOG

ARTIST	ALBUM
YEAR / COUNTRY	LABEL
CATALOG NUMBER	PRESSING VERSION

LISTENING NOTES

GRADING: SS M NM VG+ VG G+ G F P

ARTIST	ALBUM
YEAR / COUNTRY	LABEL
CATALOG NUMBER	PRESSING VERSION

LISTENING NOTES

GRADING: SS M NM VG+ VG G+ G F P

ARTIST	ALBUM
YEAR / COUNTRY	LABEL
CATALOG NUMBER	PRESSING VERSION

LISTENING NOTES

GRADING: SS M NM VG+ VG G+ G F P

ARTIST	ALBUM
YEAR / COUNTRY	LABEL
CATALOG NUMBER	PRESSING VERSION

LISTENING NOTES

GRADING: SS M NM VG+ VG G+ G F P

ARTIST	ALBUM
YEAR / COUNTRY	LABEL
CATALOG NUMBER	PRESSING VERSION

LISTENING NOTES

GRADING: SS M NM VG+ VG G+ G F P

ARTIST	ALBUM
YEAR / COUNTRY	LABEL
CATALOG NUMBER	PRESSING VERSION

LISTENING NOTES

GRADING: SS M NM VG+ VG G+ G F P

RECORD LOG

ARTIST	ALBUM
YEAR / COUNTRY	LABEL
CATALOG NUMBER	PRESSING VERSION

LISTENING NOTES

GRADING: SS M NM VG+ VG G+ G F P

ARTIST	ALBUM
YEAR / COUNTRY	LABEL
CATALOG NUMBER	PRESSING VERSION

LISTENING NOTES

GRADING: SS M NM VG+ VG G+ G F P

ARTIST	ALBUM
YEAR / COUNTRY	LABEL
CATALOG NUMBER	PRESSING VERSION

LISTENING NOTES

GRADING: SS M NM VG+ VG G+ G F P

ARTIST	ALBUM
YEAR / COUNTRY	LABEL
CATALOG NUMBER	PRESSING VERSION
LISTENING NOTES	

GRADING: SS M NM VG+ VG G+ G F P

ARTIST	ALBUM
YEAR / COUNTRY	LABEL
CATALOG NUMBER	PRESSING VERSION
LISTENING NOTES	

GRADING: SS M NM VG+ VG G+ G F P

ARTIST	ALBUM
YEAR / COUNTRY	LABEL
CATALOG NUMBER	PRESSING VERSION
LISTENING NOTES	

GRADING: SS M NM VG+ VG G+ G F P

RECORD LOG

ARTIST	ALBUM
YEAR / COUNTRY	LABEL
CATALOG NUMBER	PRESSING VERSION

LISTENING NOTES

GRADING: SS M NM VG+ VG G+ G F P

ARTIST	ALBUM
YEAR / COUNTRY	LABEL
CATALOG NUMBER	PRESSING VERSION

LISTENING NOTES

GRADING: SS M NM VG+ VG G+ G F P

ARTIST	ALBUM
YEAR / COUNTRY	LABEL
CATALOG NUMBER	PRESSING VERSION

LISTENING NOTES

GRADING: SS M NM VG+ VG G+ G F P

ARTIST	ALBUM
YEAR / COUNTRY	LABEL
CATALOG NUMBER	PRESSING VERSION

LISTENING NOTES

GRADING: SS M NM VG+ VG G+ G F P

ARTIST	ALBUM
YEAR / COUNTRY	LABEL
CATALOG NUMBER	PRESSING VERSION

LISTENING NOTES

GRADING: SS M NM VG+ VG G+ G F P

ARTIST	ALBUM
YEAR / COUNTRY	LABEL
CATALOG NUMBER	PRESSING VERSION

LISTENING NOTES

GRADING: SS M NM VG+ VG G+ G F P

RECORD LOG

ARTIST	ALBUM
YEAR / COUNTRY	LABEL
CATALOG NUMBER	PRESSING VERSION

LISTENING NOTES

GRADING: SS M NM VG+ VG G+ G F P

ARTIST	ALBUM
YEAR / COUNTRY	LABEL
CATALOG NUMBER	PRESSING VERSION

LISTENING NOTES

GRADING: SS M NM VG+ VG G+ G F P

ARTIST	ALBUM
YEAR / COUNTRY	LABEL
CATALOG NUMBER	PRESSING VERSION

LISTENING NOTES

GRADING: SS M NM VG+ VG G+ G F P

ARTIST	ALBUM
YEAR / COUNTRY	LABEL
CATALOG NUMBER	PRESSING VERSION

LISTENING NOTES

GRADING: SS M NM VG+ VG G+ G F P

ARTIST	ALBUM
YEAR / COUNTRY	LABEL
CATALOG NUMBER	PRESSING VERSION

LISTENING NOTES

GRADING: SS M NM VG+ VG G+ G F P

ARTIST	ALBUM
YEAR / COUNTRY	LABEL
CATALOG NUMBER	PRESSING VERSION

LISTENING NOTES

GRADING: SS M NM VG+ VG G+ G F P

RECORD LOG

ARTIST	ALBUM
YEAR / COUNTRY	LABEL
CATALOG NUMBER	PRESSING VERSION

LISTENING NOTES

GRADING: SS M NM VG+ VG G+ G F P

ARTIST	ALBUM
YEAR / COUNTRY	LABEL
CATALOG NUMBER	PRESSING VERSION

LISTENING NOTES

GRADING: SS M NM VG+ VG G+ G F P

ARTIST	ALBUM
YEAR / COUNTRY	LABEL
CATALOG NUMBER	PRESSING VERSION

LISTENING NOTES

GRADING: SS M NM VG+ VG G+ G F P

ARTIST	ALBUM
YEAR / COUNTRY	LABEL
CATALOG NUMBER	PRESSING VERSION

LISTENING NOTES

GRADING: SS M NM VG+ VG G+ G F P

ARTIST	ALBUM
YEAR / COUNTRY	LABEL
CATALOG NUMBER	PRESSING VERSION

LISTENING NOTES

GRADING: SS M NM VG+ VG G+ G F P

ARTIST	ALBUM
YEAR / COUNTRY	LABEL
CATALOG NUMBER	PRESSING VERSION

LISTENING NOTES

GRADING: SS M NM VG+ VG G+ G F P

RECORD LOG

ARTIST	ALBUM
YEAR / COUNTRY	LABEL
CATALOG NUMBER	PRESSING VERSION

LISTENING NOTES

GRADING: SS M NM VG+ VG G+ G F P

ARTIST	ALBUM
YEAR / COUNTRY	LABEL
CATALOG NUMBER	PRESSING VERSION

LISTENING NOTES

GRADING: SS M NM VG+ VG G+ G F P

ARTIST	ALBUM
YEAR / COUNTRY	LABEL
CATALOG NUMBER	PRESSING VERSION

LISTENING NOTES

GRADING: SS M NM VG+ VG G+ G F P

ARTIST	ALBUM
YEAR / COUNTRY	LABEL
CATALOG NUMBER	PRESSING VERSION

LISTENING NOTES

GRADING: SS M NM VG+ VG G+ G F P

ARTIST	ALBUM
YEAR / COUNTRY	LABEL
CATALOG NUMBER	PRESSING VERSION

LISTENING NOTES

GRADING: SS M NM VG+ VG G+ G F P

ARTIST	ALBUM
YEAR / COUNTRY	LABEL
CATALOG NUMBER	PRESSING VERSION

LISTENING NOTES

GRADING: SS M NM VG+ VG G+ G F P

RECORD LOG

ARTIST	ALBUM
YEAR / COUNTRY	LABEL
CATALOG NUMBER	PRESSING VERSION

LISTENING NOTES

GRADING: SS M NM VG+ VG G+ G F P

ARTIST	ALBUM
YEAR / COUNTRY	LABEL
CATALOG NUMBER	PRESSING VERSION

LISTENING NOTES

GRADING: SS M NM VG+ VG G+ G F P

ARTIST	ALBUM
YEAR / COUNTRY	LABEL
CATALOG NUMBER	PRESSING VERSION

LISTENING NOTES

GRADING: SS M NM VG+ VG G+ G F P

ARTIST	ALBUM
YEAR / COUNTRY	LABEL
CATALOG NUMBER	PRESSING VERSION

LISTENING NOTES

GRADING: SS M NM VG+ VG G+ G F P

ARTIST	ALBUM
YEAR / COUNTRY	LABEL
CATALOG NUMBER	PRESSING VERSION

LISTENING NOTES

GRADING: SS M NM VG+ VG G+ G F P

ARTIST	ALBUM
YEAR / COUNTRY	LABEL
CATALOG NUMBER	PRESSING VERSION

LISTENING NOTES

GRADING: SS M NM VG+ VG G+ G F P

RECORD LOG

ARTIST	ALBUM
YEAR / COUNTRY	LABEL
CATALOG NUMBER	PRESSING VERSION

LISTENING NOTES

GRADING: SS M NM VG+ VG G+ G F P

ARTIST	ALBUM
YEAR / COUNTRY	LABEL
CATALOG NUMBER	PRESSING VERSION

LISTENING NOTES

GRADING: SS M NM VG+ VG G+ G F P

ARTIST	ALBUM
YEAR / COUNTRY	LABEL
CATALOG NUMBER	PRESSING VERSION

LISTENING NOTES

GRADING: SS M NM VG+ VG G+ G F P

ARTIST	ALBUM
YEAR / COUNTRY	LABEL
CATALOG NUMBER	PRESSING VERSION

LISTENING NOTES

GRADING: SS M NM VG+ VG G+ G F P

ARTIST	ALBUM
YEAR / COUNTRY	LABEL
CATALOG NUMBER	PRESSING VERSION

LISTENING NOTES

GRADING: SS M NM VG+ VG G+ G F P

ARTIST	ALBUM
YEAR / COUNTRY	LABEL
CATALOG NUMBER	PRESSING VERSION

LISTENING NOTES

GRADING: SS M NM VG+ VG G+ G F P

RECORD LOG

ARTIST	ALBUM
YEAR / COUNTRY	LABEL
CATALOG NUMBER	PRESSING VERSION

LISTENING NOTES

GRADING: SS M NM VG+ VG G+ G F P

ARTIST	ALBUM
YEAR / COUNTRY	LABEL
CATALOG NUMBER	PRESSING VERSION

LISTENING NOTES

GRADING: SS M NM VG+ VG G+ G F P

ARTIST	ALBUM
YEAR / COUNTRY	LABEL
CATALOG NUMBER	PRESSING VERSION

LISTENING NOTES

GRADING: SS M NM VG+ VG G+ G F P

ARTIST	ALBUM
YEAR / COUNTRY	LABEL
CATALOG NUMBER	PRESSING VERSION

LISTENING NOTES

GRADING: SS M NM VG+ VG G+ G F P

ARTIST	ALBUM
YEAR / COUNTRY	LABEL
CATALOG NUMBER	PRESSING VERSION

LISTENING NOTES

GRADING: SS M NM VG+ VG G+ G F P

ARTIST	ALBUM
YEAR / COUNTRY	LABEL
CATALOG NUMBER	PRESSING VERSION

LISTENING NOTES

GRADING: SS M NM VG+ VG G+ G F P

RECORD LOG

ARTIST	ALBUM
YEAR / COUNTRY	LABEL
CATALOG NUMBER	PRESSING VERSION

LISTENING NOTES

GRADING: SS M NM VG+ VG G+ G F P

ARTIST	ALBUM
YEAR / COUNTRY	LABEL
CATALOG NUMBER	PRESSING VERSION

LISTENING NOTES

GRADING: SS M NM VG+ VG G+ G F P

ARTIST	ALBUM
YEAR / COUNTRY	LABEL
CATALOG NUMBER	PRESSING VERSION

LISTENING NOTES

GRADING: SS M NM VG+ VG G+ G F P

ARTIST	ALBUM
YEAR / COUNTRY	LABEL
CATALOG NUMBER	PRESSING VERSION

LISTENING NOTES

GRADING: SS M NM VG+ VG G+ G F P

ARTIST	ALBUM
YEAR / COUNTRY	LABEL
CATALOG NUMBER	PRESSING VERSION

LISTENING NOTES

GRADING: SS M NM VG+ VG G+ G F P

ARTIST	ALBUM
YEAR / COUNTRY	LABEL
CATALOG NUMBER	PRESSING VERSION

LISTENING NOTES

GRADING: SS M NM VG+ VG G+ G F P

RECORD LOG

ARTIST	ALBUM
YEAR / COUNTRY	LABEL
CATALOG NUMBER	PRESSING VERSION

LISTENING NOTES

GRADING: SS M NM VG+ VG G+ G F P

ARTIST	ALBUM
YEAR / COUNTRY	LABEL
CATALOG NUMBER	PRESSING VERSION

LISTENING NOTES

GRADING: SS M NM VG+ VG G+ G F P

ARTIST	ALBUM
YEAR / COUNTRY	LABEL
CATALOG NUMBER	PRESSING VERSION

LISTENING NOTES

GRADING: SS M NM VG+ VG G+ G F P

ARTIST	ALBUM
YEAR / COUNTRY	LABEL
CATALOG NUMBER	PRESSING VERSION

LISTENING NOTES

GRADING: SS M NM VG+ VG G+ G F P

ARTIST	ALBUM
YEAR / COUNTRY	LABEL
CATALOG NUMBER	PRESSING VERSION

LISTENING NOTES

GRADING: SS M NM VG+ VG G+ G F P

ARTIST	ALBUM
YEAR / COUNTRY	LABEL
CATALOG NUMBER	PRESSING VERSION

LISTENING NOTES

GRADING: SS M NM VG+ VG G+ G F P

RECORD LOG

ARTIST	ALBUM
YEAR / COUNTRY	LABEL
CATALOG NUMBER	PRESSING VERSION

LISTENING NOTES

GRADING: SS M NM VG+ VG G+ G F P

ARTIST	ALBUM
YEAR / COUNTRY	LABEL
CATALOG NUMBER	PRESSING VERSION

LISTENING NOTES

GRADING: SS M NM VG+ VG G+ G F P

ARTIST	ALBUM
YEAR / COUNTRY	LABEL
CATALOG NUMBER	PRESSING VERSION

LISTENING NOTES

GRADING: SS M NM VG+ VG G+ G F P

ARTIST	ALBUM
YEAR / COUNTRY	LABEL
CATALOG NUMBER	PRESSING VERSION

LISTENING NOTES

GRADING: SS M NM VG+ VG G+ G F P

ARTIST	ALBUM
YEAR / COUNTRY	LABEL
CATALOG NUMBER	PRESSING VERSION

LISTENING NOTES

GRADING: SS M NM VG+ VG G+ G F P

ARTIST	ALBUM
YEAR / COUNTRY	LABEL
CATALOG NUMBER	PRESSING VERSION

LISTENING NOTES

GRADING: SS M NM VG+ VG G+ G F P

RECORD LOG

ARTIST	ALBUM
YEAR / COUNTRY	LABEL
CATALOG NUMBER	PRESSING VERSION

LISTENING NOTES

GRADING: SS M NM VG+ VG G+ G F P

ARTIST	ALBUM
YEAR / COUNTRY	LABEL
CATALOG NUMBER	PRESSING VERSION

LISTENING NOTES

GRADING: SS M NM VG+ VG G+ G F P

ARTIST	ALBUM
YEAR / COUNTRY	LABEL
CATALOG NUMBER	PRESSING VERSION

LISTENING NOTES

GRADING: SS M NM VG+ VG G+ G F P

ARTIST	ALBUM
YEAR / COUNTRY	LABEL
CATALOG NUMBER	PRESSING VERSION

LISTENING NOTES

GRADING: SS M NM VG+ VG G+ G F P

ARTIST	ALBUM
YEAR / COUNTRY	LABEL
CATALOG NUMBER	PRESSING VERSION

LISTENING NOTES

GRADING: SS M NM VG+ VG G+ G F P

ARTIST	ALBUM
YEAR / COUNTRY	LABEL
CATALOG NUMBER	PRESSING VERSION

LISTENING NOTES

GRADING: SS M NM VG+ VG G+ G F P

RECORD LOG

ARTIST	ALBUM
YEAR / COUNTRY	LABEL
CATALOG NUMBER	PRESSING VERSION

LISTENING NOTES

GRADING: SS M NM VG+ VG G+ G F P

ARTIST	ALBUM
YEAR / COUNTRY	LABEL
CATALOG NUMBER	PRESSING VERSION

LISTENING NOTES

GRADING: SS M NM VG+ VG G+ G F P

ARTIST	ALBUM
YEAR / COUNTRY	LABEL
CATALOG NUMBER	PRESSING VERSION

LISTENING NOTES

GRADING: SS M NM VG+ VG G+ G F P

ARTIST	ALBUM
YEAR / COUNTRY	LABEL
CATALOG NUMBER	PRESSING VERSION

LISTENING NOTES

GRADING: SS M NM VG+ VG G+ G F P

ARTIST	ALBUM
YEAR / COUNTRY	LABEL
CATALOG NUMBER	PRESSING VERSION

LISTENING NOTES

GRADING: SS M NM VG+ VG G+ G F P

ARTIST	ALBUM
YEAR / COUNTRY	LABEL
CATALOG NUMBER	PRESSING VERSION

LISTENING NOTES

GRADING: SS M NM VG+ VG G+ G F P

RECORD LOG

ARTIST	ALBUM
YEAR / COUNTRY	LABEL
CATALOG NUMBER	PRESSING VERSION

LISTENING NOTES

GRADING: SS M NM VG+ VG G+ G F P

ARTIST	ALBUM
YEAR / COUNTRY	LABEL
CATALOG NUMBER	PRESSING VERSION

LISTENING NOTES

GRADING: SS M NM VG+ VG G+ G F P

ARTIST	ALBUM
YEAR / COUNTRY	LABEL
CATALOG NUMBER	PRESSING VERSION

LISTENING NOTES

GRADING: SS M NM VG+ VG G+ G F P

ARTIST	ALBUM
YEAR / COUNTRY	LABEL
CATALOG NUMBER	PRESSING VERSION

LISTENING NOTES

GRADING: SS M NM VG+ VG G+ G F P

ARTIST	ALBUM
YEAR / COUNTRY	LABEL
CATALOG NUMBER	PRESSING VERSION

LISTENING NOTES

GRADING: SS M NM VG+ VG G+ G F P

ARTIST	ALBUM
YEAR / COUNTRY	LABEL
CATALOG NUMBER	PRESSING VERSION

LISTENING NOTES

GRADING: SS M NM VG+ VG G+ G F P

RECORD LOG

ARTIST	ALBUM
YEAR / COUNTRY	LABEL
CATALOG NUMBER	PRESSING VERSION

LISTENING NOTES

GRADING: SS M NM VG+ VG G+ G F P

ARTIST	ALBUM
YEAR / COUNTRY	LABEL
CATALOG NUMBER	PRESSING VERSION

LISTENING NOTES

GRADING: SS M NM VG+ VG G+ G F P

ARTIST	ALBUM
YEAR / COUNTRY	LABEL
CATALOG NUMBER	PRESSING VERSION

LISTENING NOTES

GRADING: SS M NM VG+ VG G+ G F P

ARTIST	ALBUM
YEAR / COUNTRY	LABEL
CATALOG NUMBER	PRESSING VERSION

LISTENING NOTES

GRADING: SS M NM VG+ VG G+ G F P

ARTIST	ALBUM
YEAR / COUNTRY	LABEL
CATALOG NUMBER	PRESSING VERSION

LISTENING NOTES

GRADING: SS M NM VG+ VG G+ G F P

ARTIST	ALBUM
YEAR / COUNTRY	LABEL
CATALOG NUMBER	PRESSING VERSION

LISTENING NOTES

GRADING: SS M NM VG+ VG G+ G F P

RECORD LOG

ARTIST	ALBUM
YEAR / COUNTRY	LABEL
CATALOG NUMBER	PRESSING VERSION

LISTENING NOTES

GRADING: SS M NM VG+ VG G+ G F P

ARTIST	ALBUM
YEAR / COUNTRY	LABEL
CATALOG NUMBER	PRESSING VERSION

LISTENING NOTES

GRADING: SS M NM VG+ VG G+ G F P

ARTIST	ALBUM
YEAR / COUNTRY	LABEL
CATALOG NUMBER	PRESSING VERSION

LISTENING NOTES

GRADING: SS M NM VG+ VG G+ G F P

ARTIST	ALBUM
YEAR / COUNTRY	LABEL
CATALOG NUMBER	PRESSING VERSION

LISTENING NOTES

GRADING: SS M NM VG+ VG G+ G F P

ARTIST	ALBUM
YEAR / COUNTRY	LABEL
CATALOG NUMBER	PRESSING VERSION

LISTENING NOTES

GRADING: SS M NM VG+ VG G+ G F P

ARTIST	ALBUM
YEAR / COUNTRY	LABEL
CATALOG NUMBER	PRESSING VERSION

LISTENING NOTES

GRADING: SS M NM VG+ VG G+ G F P

RECORD LOG

ARTIST	ALBUM
YEAR / COUNTRY	LABEL
CATALOG NUMBER	PRESSING VERSION

LISTENING NOTES

GRADING: SS M NM VG+ VG G+ G F P

ARTIST	ALBUM
YEAR / COUNTRY	LABEL
CATALOG NUMBER	PRESSING VERSION

LISTENING NOTES

GRADING: SS M NM VG+ VG G+ G F P

ARTIST	ALBUM
YEAR / COUNTRY	LABEL
CATALOG NUMBER	PRESSING VERSION

LISTENING NOTES

GRADING: SS M NM VG+ VG G+ G F P

ARTIST	ALBUM
YEAR / COUNTRY	LABEL
CATALOG NUMBER	PRESSING VERSION

LISTENING NOTES

GRADING: SS M NM VG+ VG G+ G F P

ARTIST	ALBUM
YEAR / COUNTRY	LABEL
CATALOG NUMBER	PRESSING VERSION

LISTENING NOTES

GRADING: SS M NM VG+ VG G+ G F P

ARTIST	ALBUM
YEAR / COUNTRY	LABEL
CATALOG NUMBER	PRESSING VERSION

LISTENING NOTES

GRADING: SS M NM VG+ VG G+ G F P

RECORD LOG

ARTIST	ALBUM
YEAR / COUNTRY	LABEL
CATALOG NUMBER	PRESSING VERSION

LISTENING NOTES

GRADING: SS M NM VG+ VG G+ G F P

ARTIST	ALBUM
YEAR / COUNTRY	LABEL
CATALOG NUMBER	PRESSING VERSION

LISTENING NOTES

GRADING: SS M NM VG+ VG G+ G F P

ARTIST	ALBUM
YEAR / COUNTRY	LABEL
CATALOG NUMBER	PRESSING VERSION

LISTENING NOTES

GRADING: SS M NM VG+ VG G+ G F P

ARTIST	ALBUM
YEAR / COUNTRY	LABEL
CATALOG NUMBER	PRESSING VERSION

LISTENING NOTES

GRADING: SS M NM VG+ VG G+ G F P

ARTIST	ALBUM
YEAR / COUNTRY	LABEL
CATALOG NUMBER	PRESSING VERSION

LISTENING NOTES

GRADING: SS M NM VG+ VG G+ G F P

ARTIST	ALBUM
YEAR / COUNTRY	LABEL
CATALOG NUMBER	PRESSING VERSION

LISTENING NOTES

GRADING: SS M NM VG+ VG G+ G F P

RECORD LOG

ARTIST	ALBUM
YEAR / COUNTRY	LABEL
CATALOG NUMBER	PRESSING VERSION

LISTENING NOTES

GRADING: SS M NM VG+ VG G+ G F P

ARTIST	ALBUM
YEAR / COUNTRY	LABEL
CATALOG NUMBER	PRESSING VERSION

LISTENING NOTES

GRADING: SS M NM VG+ VG G+ G F P

ARTIST	ALBUM
YEAR / COUNTRY	LABEL
CATALOG NUMBER	PRESSING VERSION

LISTENING NOTES

GRADING: SS M NM VG+ VG G+ G F P

ARTIST	ALBUM
YEAR / COUNTRY	LABEL
CATALOG NUMBER	PRESSING VERSION

LISTENING NOTES

GRADING: SS M NM VG+ VG G+ G F P

ARTIST	ALBUM
YEAR / COUNTRY	LABEL
CATALOG NUMBER	PRESSING VERSION

LISTENING NOTES

GRADING: SS M NM VG+ VG G+ G F P

ARTIST	ALBUM
YEAR / COUNTRY	LABEL
CATALOG NUMBER	PRESSING VERSION

LISTENING NOTES

GRADING: SS M NM VG+ VG G+ G F P

RECORD LOG

ARTIST	ALBUM
YEAR / COUNTRY	LABEL
CATALOG NUMBER	PRESSING VERSION

LISTENING NOTES

GRADING: SS M NM VG+ VG G+ G F P

ARTIST	ALBUM
YEAR / COUNTRY	LABEL
CATALOG NUMBER	PRESSING VERSION

LISTENING NOTES

GRADING: SS M NM VG+ VG G+ G F P

ARTIST	ALBUM
YEAR / COUNTRY	LABEL
CATALOG NUMBER	PRESSING VERSION

LISTENING NOTES

GRADING: SS M NM VG+ VG G+ G F P

ARTIST	ALBUM
YEAR / COUNTRY	LABEL
CATALOG NUMBER	PRESSING VERSION

LISTENING NOTES

GRADING: SS M NM VG+ VG G+ G F P

ARTIST	ALBUM
YEAR / COUNTRY	LABEL
CATALOG NUMBER	PRESSING VERSION

LISTENING NOTES

GRADING: SS M NM VG+ VG G+ G F P

ARTIST	ALBUM
YEAR / COUNTRY	LABEL
CATALOG NUMBER	PRESSING VERSION

LISTENING NOTES

GRADING: SS M NM VG+ VG G+ G F P

RECORD LOG

ARTIST	ALBUM
YEAR / COUNTRY	LABEL
CATALOG NUMBER	PRESSING VERSION

LISTENING NOTES

GRADING: SS M NM VG+ VG G+ G F P

ARTIST	ALBUM
YEAR / COUNTRY	LABEL
CATALOG NUMBER	PRESSING VERSION

LISTENING NOTES

GRADING: SS M NM VG+ VG G+ G F P

ARTIST	ALBUM
YEAR / COUNTRY	LABEL
CATALOG NUMBER	PRESSING VERSION

LISTENING NOTES

GRADING: SS M NM VG+ VG G+ G F P

ARTIST	ALBUM
YEAR / COUNTRY	LABEL
CATALOG NUMBER	PRESSING VERSION

LISTENING NOTES

GRADING: SS M NM VG+ VG G+ G F P

ARTIST	ALBUM
YEAR / COUNTRY	LABEL
CATALOG NUMBER	PRESSING VERSION

LISTENING NOTES

GRADING: SS M NM VG+ VG G+ G F P

ARTIST	ALBUM
YEAR / COUNTRY	LABEL
CATALOG NUMBER	PRESSING VERSION

LISTENING NOTES

GRADING: SS M NM VG+ VG G+ G F P

RECORD LOG

ARTIST	ALBUM
YEAR / COUNTRY	LABEL
CATALOG NUMBER	PRESSING VERSION

LISTENING NOTES

GRADING: SS M NM VG+ VG G+ G F P

ARTIST	ALBUM
YEAR / COUNTRY	LABEL
CATALOG NUMBER	PRESSING VERSION

LISTENING NOTES

GRADING: SS M NM VG+ VG G+ G F P

ARTIST	ALBUM
YEAR / COUNTRY	LABEL
CATALOG NUMBER	PRESSING VERSION

LISTENING NOTES

GRADING: SS M NM VG+ VG G+ G F P

ARTIST	ALBUM
YEAR / COUNTRY	LABEL
CATALOG NUMBER	PRESSING VERSION

LISTENING NOTES

GRADING: SS M NM VG+ VG G+ G F P

ARTIST	ALBUM
YEAR / COUNTRY	LABEL
CATALOG NUMBER	PRESSING VERSION

LISTENING NOTES

GRADING: SS M NM VG+ VG G+ G F P

ARTIST	ALBUM
YEAR / COUNTRY	LABEL
CATALOG NUMBER	PRESSING VERSION

LISTENING NOTES

GRADING: SS M NM VG+ VG G+ G F P

RECORD LOG

ARTIST	ALBUM
YEAR / COUNTRY	LABEL
CATALOG NUMBER	PRESSING VERSION

LISTENING NOTES

GRADING: SS M NM VG+ VG G+ G F P

ARTIST	ALBUM
YEAR / COUNTRY	LABEL
CATALOG NUMBER	PRESSING VERSION

LISTENING NOTES

GRADING: SS M NM VG+ VG G+ G F P

ARTIST	ALBUM
YEAR / COUNTRY	LABEL
CATALOG NUMBER	PRESSING VERSION

LISTENING NOTES

GRADING: SS M NM VG+ VG G+ G F P

ARTIST	ALBUM
YEAR / COUNTRY	LABEL
CATALOG NUMBER	PRESSING VERSION

LISTENING NOTES

GRADING: SS M NM VG+ VG G+ G F P

ARTIST	ALBUM
YEAR / COUNTRY	LABEL
CATALOG NUMBER	PRESSING VERSION

LISTENING NOTES

GRADING: SS M NM VG+ VG G+ G F P

ARTIST	ALBUM
YEAR / COUNTRY	LABEL
CATALOG NUMBER	PRESSING VERSION

LISTENING NOTES

GRADING: SS M NM VG+ VG G+ G F P

RECORD LOG

ARTIST	ALBUM
YEAR / COUNTRY	LABEL
CATALOG NUMBER	PRESSING VERSION

LISTENING NOTES

GRADING: SS M NM VG+ VG G+ G F P

ARTIST	ALBUM
YEAR / COUNTRY	LABEL
CATALOG NUMBER	PRESSING VERSION

LISTENING NOTES

GRADING: SS M NM VG+ VG G+ G F P

ARTIST	ALBUM
YEAR / COUNTRY	LABEL
CATALOG NUMBER	PRESSING VERSION

LISTENING NOTES

GRADING: SS M NM VG+ VG G+ G F P

ARTIST	ALBUM
YEAR / COUNTRY	LABEL
CATALOG NUMBER	PRESSING VERSION

LISTENING NOTES

GRADING: SS M NM VG+ VG G+ G F P

ARTIST	ALBUM
YEAR / COUNTRY	LABEL
CATALOG NUMBER	PRESSING VERSION

LISTENING NOTES

GRADING: SS M NM VG+ VG G+ G F P

ARTIST	ALBUM
YEAR / COUNTRY	LABEL
CATALOG NUMBER	PRESSING VERSION

LISTENING NOTES

GRADING: SS M NM VG+ VG G+ G F P

RECORD LOG

ARTIST	ALBUM
YEAR / COUNTRY	LABEL
CATALOG NUMBER	PRESSING VERSION

LISTENING NOTES

GRADING: SS M NM VG+ VG G+ G F P

ARTIST	ALBUM
YEAR / COUNTRY	LABEL
CATALOG NUMBER	PRESSING VERSION

LISTENING NOTES

GRADING: SS M NM VG+ VG G+ G F P

ARTIST	ALBUM
YEAR / COUNTRY	LABEL
CATALOG NUMBER	PRESSING VERSION

LISTENING NOTES

GRADING: SS M NM VG+ VG G+ G F P

ARTIST	ALBUM
YEAR / COUNTRY	LABEL
CATALOG NUMBER	PRESSING VERSION

LISTENING NOTES

GRADING: SS M NM VG+ VG G+ G F P

ARTIST	ALBUM
YEAR / COUNTRY	LABEL
CATALOG NUMBER	PRESSING VERSION

LISTENING NOTES

GRADING: SS M NM VG+ VG G+ G F P

ARTIST	ALBUM
YEAR / COUNTRY	LABEL
CATALOG NUMBER	PRESSING VERSION

LISTENING NOTES

GRADING: SS M NM VG+ VG G+ G F P

RECORD LOG

ARTIST	ALBUM
YEAR / COUNTRY	LABEL
CATALOG NUMBER	PRESSING VERSION

LISTENING NOTES

GRADING: SS M NM VG+ VG G+ G F P

ARTIST	ALBUM
YEAR / COUNTRY	LABEL
CATALOG NUMBER	PRESSING VERSION

LISTENING NOTES

GRADING: SS M NM VG+ VG G+ G F P

ARTIST	ALBUM
YEAR / COUNTRY	LABEL
CATALOG NUMBER	PRESSING VERSION

LISTENING NOTES

GRADING: SS M NM VG+ VG G+ G F P

ARTIST	ALBUM
YEAR / COUNTRY	LABEL
CATALOG NUMBER	PRESSING VERSION

LISTENING NOTES

GRADING: SS M NM VG+ VG G+ G F P

ARTIST	ALBUM
YEAR / COUNTRY	LABEL
CATALOG NUMBER	PRESSING VERSION

LISTENING NOTES

GRADING: SS M NM VG+ VG G+ G F P

ARTIST	ALBUM
YEAR / COUNTRY	LABEL
CATALOG NUMBER	PRESSING VERSION

LISTENING NOTES

GRADING: SS M NM VG+ VG G+ G F P

RECORD LOG

ARTIST	ALBUM
YEAR / COUNTRY	LABEL
CATALOG NUMBER	PRESSING VERSION

LISTENING NOTES

GRADING: SS M NM VG+ VG G+ G F P

ARTIST	ALBUM
YEAR / COUNTRY	LABEL
CATALOG NUMBER	PRESSING VERSION

LISTENING NOTES

GRADING: SS M NM VG+ VG G+ G F P

ARTIST	ALBUM
YEAR / COUNTRY	LABEL
CATALOG NUMBER	PRESSING VERSION

LISTENING NOTES

GRADING: SS M NM VG+ VG G+ G F P

ARTIST	ALBUM
YEAR / COUNTRY	LABEL
CATALOG NUMBER	PRESSING VERSION

LISTENING NOTES

GRADING: SS M NM VG+ VG G+ G F P

ARTIST	ALBUM
YEAR / COUNTRY	LABEL
CATALOG NUMBER	PRESSING VERSION

LISTENING NOTES

GRADING: SS M NM VG+ VG G+ G F P

ARTIST	ALBUM
YEAR / COUNTRY	LABEL
CATALOG NUMBER	PRESSING VERSION

LISTENING NOTES

GRADING: SS M NM VG+ VG G+ G F P

RECORD LOG

ARTIST	ALBUM
YEAR / COUNTRY	LABEL
CATALOG NUMBER	PRESSING VERSION

LISTENING NOTES

GRADING: SS M NM VG+ VG G+ G F P

ARTIST	ALBUM
YEAR / COUNTRY	LABEL
CATALOG NUMBER	PRESSING VERSION

LISTENING NOTES

GRADING: SS M NM VG+ VG G+ G F P

ARTIST	ALBUM
YEAR / COUNTRY	LABEL
CATALOG NUMBER	PRESSING VERSION

LISTENING NOTES

GRADING: SS M NM VG+ VG G+ G F P

ARTIST	ALBUM
YEAR / COUNTRY	LABEL
CATALOG NUMBER	PRESSING VERSION

LISTENING NOTES

GRADING: SS M NM VG+ VG G+ G F P

ARTIST	ALBUM
YEAR / COUNTRY	LABEL
CATALOG NUMBER	PRESSING VERSION

LISTENING NOTES

GRADING: SS M NM VG+ VG G+ G F P

ARTIST	ALBUM
YEAR / COUNTRY	LABEL
CATALOG NUMBER	PRESSING VERSION

LISTENING NOTES

GRADING: SS M NM VG+ VG G+ G F P

RECORD LOG

ARTIST	ALBUM
YEAR / COUNTRY	LABEL
CATALOG NUMBER	PRESSING VERSION

LISTENING NOTES

GRADING: SS M NM VG+ VG G+ G F P

ARTIST	ALBUM
YEAR / COUNTRY	LABEL
CATALOG NUMBER	PRESSING VERSION

LISTENING NOTES

GRADING: SS M NM VG+ VG G+ G F P

ARTIST	ALBUM
YEAR / COUNTRY	LABEL
CATALOG NUMBER	PRESSING VERSION

LISTENING NOTES

GRADING: SS M NM VG+ VG G+ G F P

ARTIST	ALBUM
YEAR / COUNTRY	LABEL
CATALOG NUMBER	PRESSING VERSION

LISTENING NOTES

GRADING: SS M NM VG+ VG G+ G F P

ARTIST	ALBUM
YEAR / COUNTRY	LABEL
CATALOG NUMBER	PRESSING VERSION

LISTENING NOTES

GRADING: SS M NM VG+ VG G+ G F P

ARTIST	ALBUM
YEAR / COUNTRY	LABEL
CATALOG NUMBER	PRESSING VERSION

LISTENING NOTES

GRADING: SS M NM VG+ VG G+ G F P

RECORD LOG

ARTIST	ALBUM
YEAR / COUNTRY	LABEL
CATALOG NUMBER	PRESSING VERSION

LISTENING NOTES

GRADING: SS M NM VG+ VG G+ G F P

ARTIST	ALBUM
YEAR / COUNTRY	LABEL
CATALOG NUMBER	PRESSING VERSION

LISTENING NOTES

GRADING: SS M NM VG+ VG G+ G F P

ARTIST	ALBUM
YEAR / COUNTRY	LABEL
CATALOG NUMBER	PRESSING VERSION

LISTENING NOTES

GRADING: SS M NM VG+ VG G+ G F P

ARTIST	ALBUM
YEAR / COUNTRY	LABEL
CATALOG NUMBER	PRESSING VERSION

LISTENING NOTES

GRADING: SS M NM VG+ VG G+ G F P

ARTIST	ALBUM
YEAR / COUNTRY	LABEL
CATALOG NUMBER	PRESSING VERSION

LISTENING NOTES

GRADING: SS M NM VG+ VG G+ G F P

ARTIST	ALBUM
YEAR / COUNTRY	LABEL
CATALOG NUMBER	PRESSING VERSION

LISTENING NOTES

GRADING: SS M NM VG+ VG G+ G F P

RECORD LOG

ARTIST	ALBUM
YEAR / COUNTRY	LABEL
CATALOG NUMBER	PRESSING VERSION

LISTENING NOTES

GRADING: SS M NM VG+ VG G+ G F P

ARTIST	ALBUM
YEAR / COUNTRY	LABEL
CATALOG NUMBER	PRESSING VERSION

LISTENING NOTES

GRADING: SS M NM VG+ VG G+ G F P

ARTIST	ALBUM
YEAR / COUNTRY	LABEL
CATALOG NUMBER	PRESSING VERSION

LISTENING NOTES

GRADING: SS M NM VG+ VG G+ G F P

ARTIST	ALBUM
YEAR / COUNTRY	LABEL
CATALOG NUMBER	PRESSING VERSION

LISTENING NOTES

GRADING: SS M NM VG+ VG G+ G F P

ARTIST	ALBUM
YEAR / COUNTRY	LABEL
CATALOG NUMBER	PRESSING VERSION

LISTENING NOTES

GRADING: SS M NM VG+ VG G+ G F P

ARTIST	ALBUM
YEAR / COUNTRY	LABEL
CATALOG NUMBER	PRESSING VERSION

LISTENING NOTES

GRADING: SS M NM VG+ VG G+ G F P

RECORD LOG

ARTIST	ALBUM
YEAR / COUNTRY	LABEL
CATALOG NUMBER	PRESSING VERSION

LISTENING NOTES

GRADING: SS M NM VG+ VG G+ G F P

ARTIST	ALBUM
YEAR / COUNTRY	LABEL
CATALOG NUMBER	PRESSING VERSION

LISTENING NOTES

GRADING: SS M NM VG+ VG G+ G F P

ARTIST	ALBUM
YEAR / COUNTRY	LABEL
CATALOG NUMBER	PRESSING VERSION

LISTENING NOTES

GRADING: SS M NM VG+ VG G+ G F P

ARTIST	ALBUM
YEAR / COUNTRY	LABEL
CATALOG NUMBER	PRESSING VERSION

LISTENING NOTES

GRADING: SS M NM VG+ VG G+ G F P

ARTIST	ALBUM
YEAR / COUNTRY	LABEL
CATALOG NUMBER	PRESSING VERSION

LISTENING NOTES

GRADING: SS M NM VG+ VG G+ G F P

ARTIST	ALBUM
YEAR / COUNTRY	LABEL
CATALOG NUMBER	PRESSING VERSION

LISTENING NOTES

GRADING: SS M NM VG+ VG G+ G F P

RECORD LOG

ARTIST	ALBUM
YEAR / COUNTRY	LABEL
CATALOG NUMBER	PRESSING VERSION

LISTENING NOTES

GRADING: SS M NM VG+ VG G+ G F P

ARTIST	ALBUM
YEAR / COUNTRY	LABEL
CATALOG NUMBER	PRESSING VERSION

LISTENING NOTES

GRADING: SS M NM VG+ VG G+ G F P

ARTIST	ALBUM
YEAR / COUNTRY	LABEL
CATALOG NUMBER	PRESSING VERSION

LISTENING NOTES

GRADING: SS M NM VG+ VG G+ G F P

ARTIST	ALBUM
YEAR / COUNTRY	LABEL
CATALOG NUMBER	PRESSING VERSION

LISTENING NOTES

GRADING: SS M NM VG+ VG G+ G F P

ARTIST	ALBUM
YEAR / COUNTRY	LABEL
CATALOG NUMBER	PRESSING VERSION

LISTENING NOTES

GRADING: SS M NM VG+ VG G+ G F P

ARTIST	ALBUM
YEAR / COUNTRY	LABEL
CATALOG NUMBER	PRESSING VERSION

LISTENING NOTES

GRADING: SS M NM VG+ VG G+ G F P

RECORD LOG

ARTIST	ALBUM
YEAR / COUNTRY	LABEL
CATALOG NUMBER	PRESSING VERSION

LISTENING NOTES

GRADING: SS M NM VG+ VG G+ G F P

ARTIST	ALBUM
YEAR / COUNTRY	LABEL
CATALOG NUMBER	PRESSING VERSION

LISTENING NOTES

GRADING: SS M NM VG+ VG G+ G F P

ARTIST	ALBUM
YEAR / COUNTRY	LABEL
CATALOG NUMBER	PRESSING VERSION

LISTENING NOTES

GRADING: SS M NM VG+ VG G+ G F P

ARTIST	ALBUM
YEAR / COUNTRY	LABEL
CATALOG NUMBER	PRESSING VERSION

LISTENING NOTES

GRADING: SS M NM VG+ VG G+ G F P

ARTIST	ALBUM
YEAR / COUNTRY	LABEL
CATALOG NUMBER	PRESSING VERSION

LISTENING NOTES

GRADING: SS M NM VG+ VG G+ G F P

ARTIST	ALBUM
YEAR / COUNTRY	LABEL
CATALOG NUMBER	PRESSING VERSION

LISTENING NOTES

GRADING: SS M NM VG+ VG G+ G F P

RECORD LOG

ARTIST	ALBUM
YEAR / COUNTRY	LABEL
CATALOG NUMBER	PRESSING VERSION

LISTENING NOTES

GRADING: SS M NM VG+ VG G+ G F P

ARTIST	ALBUM
YEAR / COUNTRY	LABEL
CATALOG NUMBER	PRESSING VERSION

LISTENING NOTES

GRADING: SS M NM VG+ VG G+ G F P

ARTIST	ALBUM
YEAR / COUNTRY	LABEL
CATALOG NUMBER	PRESSING VERSION

LISTENING NOTES

GRADING: SS M NM VG+ VG G+ G F P

ARTIST	ALBUM
YEAR / COUNTRY	LABEL
CATALOG NUMBER	PRESSING VERSION

LISTENING NOTES

GRADING: SS M NM VG+ VG G+ G F P

ARTIST	ALBUM
YEAR / COUNTRY	LABEL
CATALOG NUMBER	PRESSING VERSION

LISTENING NOTES

GRADING: SS M NM VG+ VG G+ G F P

ARTIST	ALBUM
YEAR / COUNTRY	LABEL
CATALOG NUMBER	PRESSING VERSION

LISTENING NOTES

GRADING: SS M NM VG+ VG G+ G F P

RECORD LOG

ARTIST	ALBUM
YEAR / COUNTRY	LABEL
CATALOG NUMBER	PRESSING VERSION

LISTENING NOTES

GRADING: ○ SS ○ M ○ NM ○ VG+ ○ VG ○ G+ ○ G ○ F ○ P

ARTIST	ALBUM
YEAR / COUNTRY	LABEL
CATALOG NUMBER	PRESSING VERSION

LISTENING NOTES

GRADING: ○ SS ○ M ○ NM ○ VG+ ○ VG ○ G+ ○ G ○ F ○ P

ARTIST	ALBUM
YEAR / COUNTRY	LABEL
CATALOG NUMBER	PRESSING VERSION

LISTENING NOTES

GRADING: ○ SS ○ M ○ NM ○ VG+ ○ VG ○ G+ ○ G ○ F ○ P

ARTIST	ALBUM
YEAR / COUNTRY	LABEL
CATALOG NUMBER	PRESSING VERSION

LISTENING NOTES

GRADING: SS M NM VG+ VG G+ G F P

ARTIST	ALBUM
YEAR / COUNTRY	LABEL
CATALOG NUMBER	PRESSING VERSION

LISTENING NOTES

GRADING: SS M NM VG+ VG G+ G F P

ARTIST	ALBUM
YEAR / COUNTRY	LABEL
CATALOG NUMBER	PRESSING VERSION

LISTENING NOTES

GRADING: SS M NM VG+ VG G+ G F P

RECORD LOG

ARTIST	ALBUM
YEAR / COUNTRY	LABEL
CATALOG NUMBER	PRESSING VERSION
LISTENING NOTES	

GRADING: SS M NM VG+ VG G+ G F P

ARTIST	ALBUM
YEAR / COUNTRY	LABEL
CATALOG NUMBER	PRESSING VERSION
LISTENING NOTES	

GRADING: SS M NM VG+ VG G+ G F P

ARTIST	ALBUM
YEAR / COUNTRY	LABEL
CATALOG NUMBER	PRESSING VERSION
LISTENING NOTES	

GRADING: SS M NM VG+ VG G+ G F P

ARTIST	ALBUM
YEAR / COUNTRY	LABEL
CATALOG NUMBER	PRESSING VERSION

LISTENING NOTES

GRADING: SS M NM VG+ VG G+ G F P

ARTIST	ALBUM
YEAR / COUNTRY	LABEL
CATALOG NUMBER	PRESSING VERSION

LISTENING NOTES

GRADING: SS M NM VG+ VG G+ G F P

ARTIST	ALBUM
YEAR / COUNTRY	LABEL
CATALOG NUMBER	PRESSING VERSION

LISTENING NOTES

GRADING: SS M NM VG+ VG G+ G F P

RECORD LOG

ARTIST	ALBUM
YEAR / COUNTRY	LABEL
CATALOG NUMBER	PRESSING VERSION

LISTENING NOTES

GRADING: SS M NM VG+ VG G+ G F P

ARTIST	ALBUM
YEAR / COUNTRY	LABEL
CATALOG NUMBER	PRESSING VERSION

LISTENING NOTES

GRADING: SS M NM VG+ VG G+ G F P

ARTIST	ALBUM
YEAR / COUNTRY	LABEL
CATALOG NUMBER	PRESSING VERSION

LISTENING NOTES

GRADING: SS M NM VG+ VG G+ G F P

ARTIST	ALBUM
YEAR / COUNTRY	LABEL
CATALOG NUMBER	PRESSING VERSION

LISTENING NOTES

GRADING: SS M NM VG+ VG G+ G F P

ARTIST	ALBUM
YEAR / COUNTRY	LABEL
CATALOG NUMBER	PRESSING VERSION

LISTENING NOTES

GRADING: SS M NM VG+ VG G+ G F P

ARTIST	ALBUM
YEAR / COUNTRY	LABEL
CATALOG NUMBER	PRESSING VERSION

LISTENING NOTES

GRADING: SS M NM VG+ VG G+ G F P

RECORD LOG

ARTIST	ALBUM
YEAR / COUNTRY	LABEL
CATALOG NUMBER	PRESSING VERSION

LISTENING NOTES

GRADING: SS M NM VG+ VG G+ G F P

ARTIST	ALBUM
YEAR / COUNTRY	LABEL
CATALOG NUMBER	PRESSING VERSION

LISTENING NOTES

GRADING: SS M NM VG+ VG G+ G F P

ARTIST	ALBUM
YEAR / COUNTRY	LABEL
CATALOG NUMBER	PRESSING VERSION

LISTENING NOTES

GRADING: SS M NM VG+ VG G+ G F P

ARTIST	ALBUM
YEAR / COUNTRY	LABEL
CATALOG NUMBER	PRESSING VERSION

LISTENING NOTES

GRADING: SS M NM VG+ VG G+ G F P

ARTIST	ALBUM
YEAR / COUNTRY	LABEL
CATALOG NUMBER	PRESSING VERSION

LISTENING NOTES

GRADING: SS M NM VG+ VG G+ G F P

ARTIST	ALBUM
YEAR / COUNTRY	LABEL
CATALOG NUMBER	PRESSING VERSION

LISTENING NOTES

GRADING: SS M NM VG+ VG G+ G F P

RECORD LOG

ARTIST	ALBUM
YEAR / COUNTRY	LABEL
CATALOG NUMBER	PRESSING VERSION

LISTENING NOTES

GRADING: SS M NM VG+ VG G+ G F P

ARTIST	ALBUM
YEAR / COUNTRY	LABEL
CATALOG NUMBER	PRESSING VERSION

LISTENING NOTES

GRADING: SS M NM VG+ VG G+ G F P

ARTIST	ALBUM
YEAR / COUNTRY	LABEL
CATALOG NUMBER	PRESSING VERSION

LISTENING NOTES

GRADING: SS M NM VG+ VG G+ G F P

ARTIST	ALBUM
YEAR / COUNTRY	LABEL
CATALOG NUMBER	PRESSING VERSION

LISTENING NOTES

GRADING: SS M NM VG+ VG G+ G F P

ARTIST	ALBUM
YEAR / COUNTRY	LABEL
CATALOG NUMBER	PRESSING VERSION

LISTENING NOTES

GRADING: SS M NM VG+ VG G+ G F P

ARTIST	ALBUM
YEAR / COUNTRY	LABEL
CATALOG NUMBER	PRESSING VERSION

LISTENING NOTES

GRADING: SS M NM VG+ VG G+ G F P

RECORD LOG

ARTIST	ALBUM
YEAR / COUNTRY	LABEL
CATALOG NUMBER	PRESSING VERSION

LISTENING NOTES

GRADING: SS M NM VG+ VG G+ G F P

ARTIST	ALBUM
YEAR / COUNTRY	LABEL
CATALOG NUMBER	PRESSING VERSION

LISTENING NOTES

GRADING: SS M NM VG+ VG G+ G F P

ARTIST	ALBUM
YEAR / COUNTRY	LABEL
CATALOG NUMBER	PRESSING VERSION

LISTENING NOTES

GRADING: SS M NM VG+ VG G+ G F P

ARTIST	ALBUM
YEAR / COUNTRY	LABEL
CATALOG NUMBER	PRESSING VERSION

LISTENING NOTES

GRADING: SS M NM VG+ VG G+ G F P

ARTIST	ALBUM
YEAR / COUNTRY	LABEL
CATALOG NUMBER	PRESSING VERSION

LISTENING NOTES

GRADING: SS M NM VG+ VG G+ G F P

ARTIST	ALBUM
YEAR / COUNTRY	LABEL
CATALOG NUMBER	PRESSING VERSION

LISTENING NOTES

GRADING: SS M NM VG+ VG G+ G F P

RECORD LOG

ARTIST	ALBUM
YEAR / COUNTRY	LABEL
CATALOG NUMBER	PRESSING VERSION

LISTENING NOTES

GRADING: SS M NM VG+ VG G+ G F P

ARTIST	ALBUM
YEAR / COUNTRY	LABEL
CATALOG NUMBER	PRESSING VERSION

LISTENING NOTES

GRADING: SS M NM VG+ VG G+ G F P

ARTIST	ALBUM
YEAR / COUNTRY	LABEL
CATALOG NUMBER	PRESSING VERSION

LISTENING NOTES

GRADING: SS M NM VG+ VG G+ G F P

ARTIST	ALBUM
YEAR / COUNTRY	LABEL
CATALOG NUMBER	PRESSING VERSION

LISTENING NOTES

GRADING: SS M NM VG+ VG G+ G F P

ARTIST	ALBUM
YEAR / COUNTRY	LABEL
CATALOG NUMBER	PRESSING VERSION

LISTENING NOTES

GRADING: SS M NM VG+ VG G+ G F P

ARTIST	ALBUM
YEAR / COUNTRY	LABEL
CATALOG NUMBER	PRESSING VERSION

LISTENING NOTES

GRADING: SS M NM VG+ VG G+ G F P

RECORD LOG

ARTIST	ALBUM
YEAR / COUNTRY	LABEL
CATALOG NUMBER	PRESSING VERSION

LISTENING NOTES

GRADING: SS M NM VG+ VG G+ G F P

ARTIST	ALBUM
YEAR / COUNTRY	LABEL
CATALOG NUMBER	PRESSING VERSION

LISTENING NOTES

GRADING: SS M NM VG+ VG G+ G F P

ARTIST	ALBUM
YEAR / COUNTRY	LABEL
CATALOG NUMBER	PRESSING VERSION

LISTENING NOTES

GRADING: SS M NM VG+ VG G+ G F P

ARTIST	ALBUM
YEAR / COUNTRY	LABEL
CATALOG NUMBER	PRESSING VERSION

LISTENING NOTES

GRADING: SS M NM VG+ VG G+ G F P

ARTIST	ALBUM
YEAR / COUNTRY	LABEL
CATALOG NUMBER	PRESSING VERSION

LISTENING NOTES

GRADING: SS M NM VG+ VG G+ G F P

ARTIST	ALBUM
YEAR / COUNTRY	LABEL
CATALOG NUMBER	PRESSING VERSION

LISTENING NOTES

GRADING: SS M NM VG+ VG G+ G F P

RECORD LOG

ARTIST	ALBUM
YEAR / COUNTRY	LABEL
CATALOG NUMBER	PRESSING VERSION

LISTENING NOTES

GRADING: SS M NM VG+ VG G+ G F P

ARTIST	ALBUM
YEAR / COUNTRY	LABEL
CATALOG NUMBER	PRESSING VERSION

LISTENING NOTES

GRADING: SS M NM VG+ VG G+ G F P

ARTIST	ALBUM
YEAR / COUNTRY	LABEL
CATALOG NUMBER	PRESSING VERSION

LISTENING NOTES

GRADING: SS M NM VG+ VG G+ G F P

ARTIST	ALBUM
YEAR / COUNTRY	LABEL
CATALOG NUMBER	PRESSING VERSION

LISTENING NOTES

GRADING: SS M NM VG+ VG G+ G F P

ARTIST	ALBUM
YEAR / COUNTRY	LABEL
CATALOG NUMBER	PRESSING VERSION

LISTENING NOTES

GRADING: SS M NM VG+ VG G+ G F P

ARTIST	ALBUM
YEAR / COUNTRY	LABEL
CATALOG NUMBER	PRESSING VERSION

LISTENING NOTES

GRADING: SS M NM VG+ VG G+ G F P

RECORD LOG

ARTIST	ALBUM
YEAR / COUNTRY	LABEL
CATALOG NUMBER	PRESSING VERSION

LISTENING NOTES

GRADING: SS M NM VG+ VG G+ G F P

ARTIST	ALBUM
YEAR / COUNTRY	LABEL
CATALOG NUMBER	PRESSING VERSION

LISTENING NOTES

GRADING: SS M NM VG+ VG G+ G F P

ARTIST	ALBUM
YEAR / COUNTRY	LABEL
CATALOG NUMBER	PRESSING VERSION

LISTENING NOTES

GRADING: SS M NM VG+ VG G+ G F P

ARTIST	ALBUM
YEAR / COUNTRY	LABEL
CATALOG NUMBER	PRESSING VERSION

LISTENING NOTES

GRADING: SS M NM VG+ VG G+ G F P

ARTIST	ALBUM
YEAR / COUNTRY	LABEL
CATALOG NUMBER	PRESSING VERSION

LISTENING NOTES

GRADING: SS M NM VG+ VG G+ G F P

ARTIST	ALBUM
YEAR / COUNTRY	LABEL
CATALOG NUMBER	PRESSING VERSION

LISTENING NOTES

GRADING: SS M NM VG+ VG G+ G F P

RECORD LOG

ARTIST	ALBUM
YEAR / COUNTRY	LABEL
CATALOG NUMBER	PRESSING VERSION

LISTENING NOTES

GRADING: SS M NM VG+ VG G+ G F P

ARTIST	ALBUM
YEAR / COUNTRY	LABEL
CATALOG NUMBER	PRESSING VERSION

LISTENING NOTES

GRADING: SS M NM VG+ VG G+ G F P

ARTIST	ALBUM
YEAR / COUNTRY	LABEL
CATALOG NUMBER	PRESSING VERSION

LISTENING NOTES

GRADING: SS M NM VG+ VG G+ G F P

ARTIST	ALBUM
YEAR / COUNTRY	LABEL
CATALOG NUMBER	PRESSING VERSION

LISTENING NOTES

GRADING: SS M NM VG+ VG G+ G F P

ARTIST	ALBUM
YEAR / COUNTRY	LABEL
CATALOG NUMBER	PRESSING VERSION

LISTENING NOTES

GRADING: SS M NM VG+ VG G+ G F P

ARTIST	ALBUM
YEAR / COUNTRY	LABEL
CATALOG NUMBER	PRESSING VERSION

LISTENING NOTES

GRADING: SS M NM VG+ VG G+ G F P

RECORD LOG

ARTIST	ALBUM
YEAR / COUNTRY	LABEL
CATALOG NUMBER	PRESSING VERSION

LISTENING NOTES

GRADING: SS M NM VG+ VG G+ G F P

ARTIST	ALBUM
YEAR / COUNTRY	LABEL
CATALOG NUMBER	PRESSING VERSION

LISTENING NOTES

GRADING: SS M NM VG+ VG G+ G F P

ARTIST	ALBUM
YEAR / COUNTRY	LABEL
CATALOG NUMBER	PRESSING VERSION

LISTENING NOTES

GRADING: SS M NM VG+ VG G+ G F P

ARTIST	ALBUM
YEAR / COUNTRY	LABEL
CATALOG NUMBER	PRESSING VERSION

LISTENING NOTES

GRADING: SS M NM VG+ VG G+ G F P

ARTIST	ALBUM
YEAR / COUNTRY	LABEL
CATALOG NUMBER	PRESSING VERSION

LISTENING NOTES

GRADING: SS M NM VG+ VG G+ G F P

ARTIST	ALBUM
YEAR / COUNTRY	LABEL
CATALOG NUMBER	PRESSING VERSION

LISTENING NOTES

GRADING: SS M NM VG+ VG G+ G F P

RECORD LOG

ARTIST	ALBUM
YEAR / COUNTRY	LABEL
CATALOG NUMBER	PRESSING VERSION

LISTENING NOTES

GRADING: SS M NM VG+ VG G+ G F P

ARTIST	ALBUM
YEAR / COUNTRY	LABEL
CATALOG NUMBER	PRESSING VERSION

LISTENING NOTES

GRADING: SS M NM VG+ VG G+ G F P

ARTIST	ALBUM
YEAR / COUNTRY	LABEL
CATALOG NUMBER	PRESSING VERSION

LISTENING NOTES

GRADING: SS M NM VG+ VG G+ G F P

ARTIST	ALBUM
YEAR / COUNTRY	LABEL
CATALOG NUMBER	PRESSING VERSION

LISTENING NOTES

GRADING: SS M NM VG+ VG G+ G F P

ARTIST	ALBUM
YEAR / COUNTRY	LABEL
CATALOG NUMBER	PRESSING VERSION

LISTENING NOTES

GRADING: SS M NM VG+ VG G+ G F P

ARTIST	ALBUM
YEAR / COUNTRY	LABEL
CATALOG NUMBER	PRESSING VERSION

LISTENING NOTES

GRADING: SS M NM VG+ VG G+ G F P

RECORD LOG

ARTIST	ALBUM
YEAR / COUNTRY	LABEL
CATALOG NUMBER	PRESSING VERSION

LISTENING NOTES

GRADING: ○ SS ○ M ○ NM ○ VG+ ○ VG ○ G+ ○ G ○ F ○ P

ARTIST	ALBUM
YEAR / COUNTRY	LABEL
CATALOG NUMBER	PRESSING VERSION

LISTENING NOTES

GRADING: ○ SS ○ M ○ NM ○ VG+ ○ VG ○ G+ ○ G ○ F ○ P

ARTIST	ALBUM
YEAR / COUNTRY	LABEL
CATALOG NUMBER	PRESSING VERSION

LISTENING NOTES

GRADING: ○ SS ○ M ○ NM ○ VG+ ○ VG ○ G+ ○ G ○ F ○ P

ARTIST	ALBUM
YEAR / COUNTRY	LABEL
CATALOG NUMBER	PRESSING VERSION

LISTENING NOTES

GRADING: SS M NM VG+ VG G+ G F P

ARTIST	ALBUM
YEAR / COUNTRY	LABEL
CATALOG NUMBER	PRESSING VERSION

LISTENING NOTES

GRADING: SS M NM VG+ VG G+ G F P

ARTIST	ALBUM
YEAR / COUNTRY	LABEL
CATALOG NUMBER	PRESSING VERSION

LISTENING NOTES

GRADING: SS M NM VG+ VG G+ G F P

Index